Homework Heroes

Drew and Cynthia Johnson

with Introduction by

Priscilla L. Vail, M. A. T.

KAPLAN BOOKS

New York   London   Toronto   Sydney   Singapore

Kaplan Publishing
Published by Simon & Schuster, Inc.
1230 Avenue of the Americas
New York, NY 10020

For bulk sales to schools, colleges, and universities, please contact:
Order Department, Simon & Schuster, Inc., 100 Front Street,
Riverside, NJ 08075. Phone: (800) 223-2336. Fax: (800) 943-9831.

For information regarding special discounts for other bulk purchases,
please contact Simon & Schuster Special Sales at 1-800-456-6798 or
business@simonandschuster.com

Editor: Beth Grupper
Cover Design: Cheung Tai
Interior Design: Richard Oriolo
Interior Layout and Production: Anaxos, Inc.

Manufactured in the United States of America

January 2002
10 9 8 7 6 5 4 3 2 1

Library of Congress Cataloging-in-Publication Data

ISBN: 0-7432-2259-8

Table of Contents

Chapter 1: Developing Good Homework Habits

Chapter 2: A Review of Key Junior High

Math Concepts

Chapter 3: A Review of Key Junior High

 English Concepts

Chapter 4: A Review of Key Junior High

Science Concepts

Homework Heroes: Grades 6-8

HOMEWORK IS A FACT OF life for most children, but parents are often confused about their role in this daily drama and concerned about meshing homework with the general dynamics of personal and family life. While homework is sometimes a source of frustration and argument, it can also be a vehicle for cooperation, a source of pride and accomplishment, and an opportunity for fun and creativity.

Fantasy? No.

From my own experiences as a full-time teacher for over a quarter of a century, a parent of four children, a grandmother of six, a student of learning, a curriculum planner, and a designer and leader of teacher and parenting workshops across this country and abroad, I have some:

complexities to explore and strategies to share

cautions to mention and techniques to offer

issues to highlight and research to quarry

questions to raise and purposes to reinforce

These combinations can help you and your child reduce negatives to a minimum and enhance the positive aspects of a daily reality. You can be Homework Heroes to one another, and this book is designed to set you on your way.

If you have read some of my books or articles, or have heard me speak, some of what follows here may sound familiar. Good, that means we are already friends. For new acquaintances, my message is both realistic and optimistic:

Your child can succeed.

You can survive.

There is life after homework.

Percolate and Prepare

Well-planned homework in grades 6-8 helps students percolate and prepare. Because their school schedules push them relentlessly from one subject to another—each with its own vocabulary—students benefit from homework time as a chance to sift through what they are learning and let new information join with old in personal, therefore permanent, ways. They also can use homework time as a way to prepare for class discussions. Percolate and prepare.

Obviously, students at this level also need to have solidified the skills from earlier levels. It is dangerous to climb a ladder skipping rungs.

Students in grades 6-8 are cusp-sitters, trying to figure out whether they are adults or children. Those who teach them and raise them are both flame keepers and flame tamers. In spite of sophisticated terminology (frequently sexual) many of these young people are internally chaotic and immature. Thus, adults in their lives must remember to reach to the heart as well as teach to the head.

Pediatrician and author Mel Levine says that the governing agenda for students this age is "the avoidance of humiliation at all costs." For example, some would rather receive a zero than hand in written work if it's likely to come back looking like a patient from the emergency room, slashed with red marks. One seventh-grader said, "All I get back are bleeding beasts. It's embarrassing." One kid might become the class clown to disguise his poor reading. Another might try to apply such social skills as cooperation, politeness, and flattery to intimidating intellectual challenges. These are ages of blunt honesty and close concealment. Adults need to accept the former and penetrate the latter.

A word to the wise: provide those structures and examples of orderliness that show children how to organize themselves. (See page 13.) Parents who say with barely concealed pride, "I'm *never* on time," are hobbling their offspring. Anyone can learn to be organized. The key is wanting to. You owe this to your child.

Here are twenty questions you need to address as you think about homework. This structure will provide a banister to support and guide us as we walk our way up through this sometimes conflict-ridden topic.

1. What is the homework policy at your child's school?

2. What is each individual teacher's homework policy?

3. What is your homework policy as a parent?

4. Who has ownership of homework?

5. How does homework solidify or undermine eight relationships?

6. Time: Does your child use it well?

7. Space: Where is homework to be done?

8. Do you have a Time and Space Homework Pact?

9. How long should homework take?

10. What about boredom and drudgery?

11. Does your child have the prerequisite reading skills to manage assigned homework?

12. Do your child's developmental and language levels match the assigned tasks?

13. Do your child's handwriting skills match the assigned tasks?

14. Do your child's study skills and learning styles match the assigned tasks?

15. What if your child has dyslexia or learning disabilities?

16. Are your child's emotional habits and considerations taken into account?

17. Do your child's memory skills match the requirements of the homework?

18. Does the homework attach new concepts to ones that are already familiar?

19. Does your child's homework promote privacy, participation, and enjoying your kid?

20. Do you watch the "Plimsoll Line"? (No, it's not a new television show. Puzzled? Read on!)

Let's look at these twenty questions, one by one, and explore their implications for children in grades 6-8.

1. What is the homework policy at your child's school?

If homework is going to demand the amount of time schools expect and require, the school philosophy should be clear and articulated. Is homework for:

reinforcement of concepts?

extension of concepts?

preparation for concepts?

development of independent learning?

enjoyment and expansion of creativity?

drill and practice, including test preparation?

time filling?

Some schools have a punitive "it's time to make grown-ups out of them" attitude, strikingly at variance with the nature of kids this age. Teachers at these levels may say, "We've got to get them ready for high school." No. Their job is to help students be really good middle schoolers. These are golden years for expansion of imagination, making strong connections across disciplines, assimilating information, and *thinking!*

You have every right to ask for, encourage, or even demand a statement from the school on its homework philosophy: who, what, when, where, why, and how.

Since many schools have not articulated such a policy, it may take a little time and "cajoling," but parents should never underestimate the power a coordinated group wields. If such a statement is not in place, or in writing, it is reasonable for parents to ask the administration when they would be able to have one ready: next week, next month, three months? What would they like you and other parents to do in the meantime? Parents (and students) deserve this information. Be polite but firm, while remembering that schools, like most institutions, move at a glacial pace.

2. What is each individual teacher's homework policy? Are each teacher's ideas consistent with what the school has stated, and among each other?

By sixth grade your child's education is probably departmentalized—a different teacher for each subject. If teachers from different disciplines don't coordinate, students can get caught in an overlap overload of schoolwork. A well-considered school policy may save lives!

Some teachers feel, "My discipline is the one that matters most, therefore I'm entitled to give the most homework." Or a teacher may say, "This unit is so important, I'll just add on twenty minutes to the homework." This twenty minutes may turn into forty minutes for some students, and other teachers may be doing the same thing. Thus your child may not be burning the midnight oil, but rather the morning oil. The poor soul is late for school before even getting to bed.

Such urgency teaches the lesson that expectations are impossible to meet, which, in turn, teaches students to stay on the surface, cut corners, slide by, or bite their fingernails up to their shoulders.

If your child is caught in a crunch, first talk to the teacher(s) involved. If you need to go further, make an appointment with the administrator. Base your comments on what the school has stated as homework policy. This will be much more effective than what might be interpreted as "whining about Johnny."

3. What is your homework policy as a parent?

Many children at this level have active after-school lives. Simultaneously, the volume of homework increases and long-term projects enter the scene. One mother said to me, "Job? I've got three kids. I've got *homework!* How could I have a job?"

As a parent, you need to articulate your family homework policy. For example, one family I know says, "During the week, we all have our routines for homework, bedtime, and adult responsibilities. When the weekend comes, we need to have time for fun together, but we still have chores and homework. For us, Saturday is the time to do them. Adults do the errands and transport kids to athletic games or practices. Our kids do their homework, even if it means they have to get up early. By the end of the day, the chores are done, the homework is finished, and we can go out for supper, hit the movies, rent a video, or have friends over. It's important to give fun an important place on the schedule."

Although this requires you to think through the issue and explain the family policy up front, the resulting benefits and freedom from nagging are worth the effort.

Here are some direct quotes from parents who feel they have worked out homework issues well:

> "Parents should be aware of how much of a distraction a computer is. Even parents who use computers at work don't realize how hard it is for kids to sit down at a computer for schoolwork and use it only as an educational tool. E-mailing is fun but it's a huge time waster. When parents talk with their kids about limiting computer use, they usually only talk about safety, but they also need to set limits on e-mail to friends and instant messaging during homework time. And unless the parents have a pact with their kids, with one mouse click, your kid is out of school work and into chats with friends."

"Lots of parents in our district are trimming back after-school activities. The kids have one already . . . homework. Lots of families are allowing one more. Period. And many families have an ironclad no weekday TV rule. After a little initial balking the kids are fine. And it's amazing how much discretionary time that adds into a child's day!"

4. Who has ownership of homework?

Let there be no fuzziness here: your child owns and is responsible for the assignments; your child is the one to do the work. Let your child own the triumphs. Anything else is theft.

Does this mean no help? Of course not. You should help by providing the time and space in which to work on assignments, offering encouragement, listening to spelling words, admiring a product, praising diligence, helping to sound out an unfamiliar word, or talking through the layout of a history project. Yes, you should be interested and supportive, but your child owns the homework. At this age, you should be available for organization and pre-planning, but then step back.

If, in spite of the Time and Space Treaty (see question 8) and help with pre-planning, your child blows off the assignment or hasn't gotten the source material, your child owns the problem. Being clear about ownership allows your child to feel the positive or negative consequences of personal behavior. Sounds mean? Habitual last-minute rescue teaches dependency and reinforces procrastination, both of which make trouble in the real world.

5. How does homework solidify or undermine eight relationships?

parent/child	child/parent
parent/teacher	child/teacher
parent/family	child/family
parent/self	child/self

Understanding how these relationships interconnect, and being sure all are in good repair, separately and jointly, is fundamental to effective vigilance, your privilege as a parent.

In the **parent/child** homework relationship, you have six opportunities: back off; foster independence; encourage autonomy; let consequences follow behaviors; don't try to be your child's chief crusader, savior, or martyr (remember, Joan of Arc got burned at the end); and establish and model the treaty model outlined in question 8.

Because of academic demands at this age, you may need to take your child to the library over the weekend or make a quick shopping trip for vital materials. Do it, smiling.

In the **child/parent** homework relationship, your child should be working to establish feelings of responsibility, diligence without dependency, and pride in accomplishment.

During these years, your child is entering that confusing relationship with parents made of equal parts admiration and loathing; you are a source of great pride and deep embarrassment. Hormones are starting to work. This means you will be both needed and unwelcome. Summon all your tact and diplomatic skills while providing support and benevolent neglect. Do not let homework become a battlefield for displaced emotions.

In the **parent/teacher** homework relationship, you should ask teachers these questions:

What are your goals for this year?

How can we help achieve them?

How do you want us to contact you if necessary?

How do you want us to deal with overload or errors we see our child making?

You need to meet and talk with all your child's teachers now that there isn't just one homeroom teacher. If it seems likely that issues will emerge as the year unfolds, establish a check-in schedule in September or at the beginning of each semester.

If your child has an issue or a problem, address it *early*. Be frank. If problems surface, speak up sooner rather than later.

When talking with a teacher, be up front and cooperative, descriptive instead of critical, and *never* pounce on a teacher in the hall or at the door of the classroom as the period is starting. The teacher's proper focus is on the group: orchestrating the class, drawing the group into the lesson, generating excitement, soothing feelings, and infusing courage. Diverting the teacher's attention at such a time is like delivering a telephone message to a conductor about to raise the baton. Instead, send a note saying what you want to talk about, how much time you think you need, and suggest a time or ask the teacher to set an alternative.

In the **child/teacher** homework relationship, your child needs to be honest with the teacher. Your child needs to tell the teacher if his homework routinely takes too long. False bravery builds unrealistic expectations. When your child is honest, the teacher can do what teachers go into teaching to do: help.

Your child also needs to develop skills of self-advocacy: "I have trouble listening and writing at the same time. Could you please write the assignment on the board for me to copy, so I will get it down correctly?" Self-advocacy needs to come at the very beginning of the term or semester, not after two disappointing tests scores.

If the teacher asks the students to study from notes taken in class, or from the board, it is the teacher's job to teach note-taking, not just expect it. It is fair for your child to ask the teacher to check over any notes to be used for studying if he feels he needs extra help.

In the **parent/family** homework relationship, you are the coordinator and producer of the show, integrating each child's needs, and coordinating demands for attention with the competing needs of siblings, spouse, the dog, or a grandparent. (Being a grandparent myself allows me to use that sequence.) You should be sure to plan a quiet time. All family members need collective peace as well as collective urgency. You can establish this priority.

In the **child/family** homework relationship, insofar as possible, your child should do homework with its attendant demands for help, quiet and so forth, when others in the family are similarly engaged. This means that each child in a family should have an ample supply of enjoyable projects to do solo while others are working. Remember, too, that your child can give help as well as receive it. Two-way streets make for even traffic flow. Your sixth-, seventh-, or eighth-grader can help a sibling, or even a parent!

In the **parent/self** homework relationship, learn something new yourself: tai chi, how to make a soufflé, how to hit an overhead smash, how to play an instrument, speak Spanish, or read the financial page of the newspaper. Let your child see you trying, flubbing, retrying, and enjoying . . . and maybe even succeeding. Every time you look in the mirror, you should see someone with increasing capabilities. Don't live vicariously, and especially don't try to live vicariously through your child's homework. *You* are not getting the grade.

In the **student/self** homework relationship, your child needs to block in some personal and down time. These must have honorable slots on the calendar and be as sacred as other regularly scheduled events.

6. Time: Does your child use it well?

Does your child understand the concept of "elapsing time," meaning how long something takes to do, and how that fits into the time allowance provided for the task? There are literally MILLIONS of adults who have destroyed potentially satisfying personal and business relationships because they never developed the concept of elapsing time. If you don't have the concept, you can't monitor it. If you can't monitor it, it is not part of your planning apparatus. You lose, big time.

Here is a simple, free, effective strategy for teaching elapsing time: Say to your child, "Look at the clock when you start to do your home-work. When you think ten minutes has gone by, look up at the clock. Are you early, late, or on the money? Do this for five days. You will begin to see your own pattern. If you are usually early, try to stretch out your sense of ten minutes. If you are usually late, try to rein it in. If you are usually on the money, can you predict 30 minutes?"

Have your child move from ten minutes to thirty and then to an hour. Try three hours. A child who can do this develops an internal alarm clock that will be helpful in getting places on time and also fitting work into time slots allotted for it. When a teacher says, "Write for the next thirty minutes on a memorable experience," the internal timer will tick, allowing her to pace herself so she finishes in the allotted time.

This works in real life as well as in homework. If you are due to leave in an hour, do you have a sense of how much time is left before you need to get dressed? Grownups can practice this skill, too.

Once the concept of elapsing time is jelled, you can help your child with what is technically called "projected time." For example, you, as an adult, need to be able to predict how long it will take to fold the laundry, make the salad, balance the checkbook, and jog two miles; or to organize a spreadsheet, make a summary of the morning's two meetings, and call two clients. Similarly, your child needs to estimate how long it will take to learn the spelling words, make the mask for the play, put the equipment in the soccer bag, and practice the trombone. Teach your child to make an estimate, do the tasks, and check on the estimate. Adjust accordingly the next time.

A truth: predicting required time depends on recognizing the passing of time.

7. Space: Where is homework to be done?

It is important for you to identify, guarantee, and equip a place for your child to work, encouraging your child to give it a name: Homework Heaven, the Studying Spot, or the Serious Desk. Your child should establish the habit of going there to do homework, leaving when the job is done. It should *not* be in front of the television!

It is important for you and your child to acknowledge that surroundings influence concentration and focus . . . as well as their opposites. Some places are designed for fun and relaxation. Your child needs to choose the setting according to the purpose.

By the time children reach grades 6-8, they have more stuff than they had when they were younger. Therefore, they need tighter organization and a bigger, well-defined study area. Most children this age profit from color-coding: red folder for math, green for science, and so forth. Use these colors to annotate the home/work calendar. You can read more about this in the following section.

8. Do you have a Time and Space Homework Pact?

You and your child should settle on a Time and Space Homework Pact, a family policy of when and where homework is to be done. To craft such a pact, you and your child need to agree on these two aspects of homework planning while taking into account student preferences and family realities.

First, let's think about the time aspect of the pact. Your child may want to sit right down after school and polish off the homework. Or he may need to have something to eat, play with the guinea pig, skip rope, or log on to the computer for a while before revisiting academics. If your child has an after-school activity on Tuesdays and Thursdays, he may need to have supper first on those evenings and then tackle the homework. He also needs to decide whether to try to do all the homework at one sitting, or break it into chunks. If you agree on the latter, does he want to do the hard subjects first, saving the easier ones for later, or vice versa? If the pact is going to work, it must reflect and include your child's individual needs and preferences.

Regarding space, your child may like to do homework in the bedroom. But if he is like many others, the bedroom has connotations of drifting and dreaming. That atmosphere may override the purposefulness studying requires. If so, he may do better studying in the living room, the den, or at the kitchen table. No single answer is right for all children. Take your home environment and your child's preferences into account.

Many families with children this age fight over whether or not the child should (can?) study with music playing. Some children claim they do better with beats and rhythms in their heads. Some parents don't care. Other children need quiet. Some parents need silence in order to concentrate. Many brain surgeons operate to rock music. If this is an issue in your family, try it one way for six weeks and the other way for the next six weeks. Which six weeks got the best results?

When all the issues have been fleshed out, you and your child need to agree on the rules, and then write and sign a treaty that will remain in effect for six weeks. During these six weeks there will be no further discussion of whens and wheres. After that, all issues can be renegotiated. This fair and comprehensive approach eliminates nightly bargaining, which is a great relief to all concerned.

Major tools for the Time and Space Treaty are the three C's: clock, calendar, and color-coding.

First, be sure your child really knows how to tell time. Some kids in grades 6-8 appear to know how because they call off the numbers on their digital watches. This surface skill may mask an underlying confusion. Be sure your child can use an analog watch and clock. Why? A digital timepiece shows only the present moment, giving no indication of what came before or what is around the corner. Planning requires a sense of past, present, and future. If your child can actively plan his homework, he can feel in charge. If your child doesn't have the tools for planning, he is a constant victim; homework is something that happens to him instead of something he makes happen. It is important to check on this skill now.

You and your child, together, need to color-code the calendar, marking in whatever colors you have chosen to represent regular events such as music lessons or athletic practices, long-term assignments, and special upcoming items such as holidays, birthdays, or vacations. If a two-week science project is assigned, have your child put it on the calendar in the appropriate color. Mark the date the project was assigned and the completion date. Mark the halfway date. Talk over with your child what needs to be completed by the halfway date in order for him to complete the task on time.

A sample pact for this age might say:

> Homework time will be divided into two sections: one after sports and just before supper, one immediately after supper. Homework will be done at the desk in the den and these times will be uninterrupted by phone calls or e-mail. Our goals are that supper will be delicious and homework will be completed within the projected time.
>
> This pact will remain in effect until _____(date).
> Signed: _____
> (your child)
>
> _____
> (you)
> Date:_____

Post the pact on the refrigerator door, the family bulletin board, or some other serious, public place.

It goes without saying that you, as a parent, must model the behaviors you expect from your child. It's not fair to say "Oops. I forgot! We have to go out in the car. How about doing your homework on the back seat, and I'll buy you a bag of chips and a soda to make it more pleasant?"

You and your child may want to share this treaty with the teachers who, ideally, will bless and cooperate with the endeavor.

9. How long should homework take?

If your child's school policy says that sixth-grade homework is expected to take fifty or sixty minutes but your child is spending seventy, eighty, or ninety minutes (or variations thereof), is it because the teacher's time estimates are short?

With students this age, it is important to assess whether assignments take too long because of known or undetected difficulties with reading, unreliable reading comprehension skills, interrupted concentration and daydreaming, or poor planning. We will address these issues in more detail in subsequent sections.

If homework is too hard or takes too long, you, or you and your child together, should be open with the teachers as suggested in earlier sections. In preparation for such conversations, you and your child should keep a nightly log of genuine TOT (Time on Task) *vs.* "book holding."

10. What about boredom and drudgery?

Sometimes, to save face, children say, "I'm bored," or "This is boring," when they really mean, "I'm scared I can't do this," or "This is too hard." In such cases, the trick is to get right at the problem, break down the task, and help with whatever components are getting in the way. The longer the masquerade continues, the harder it is to get the real, necessary job done.

Real boredom is a problem when teachers assign worksheets of tasks the child has already mastered. In such cases, you might say to the teacher, "Sam is very good at diagramming sentences, but gets bogged down if he has to do fifty a night. Would it be possible for him to do every other one, or half of them, and use the extra time for a project?"

And then there's drudgery. Every exciting subject has underpinnings of drudgery. Neurosurgeons have memorized anatomy; astrophysicists learned formulae. Acquiring this knowledge is drudgery, and not all homework can be fun. Just as dribble practice leads to good basketball techniques, your child needs to learn and rehearse facts and procedures. The need for solid foundations requires that your child will have to do some memorization, repetition, and intellectual setting-up exercises. That's life.

With luck, with a creative teacher, or with some requests from you and your child, lots of the homework for this age can be in the form of projects. Projects harness learning, invite connections, and release creativity. The beginning of a term or semester is the ideal time to ask about the relationship of homework and projects.

11. Does your child have the prerequisite reading skills to manage assigned homework?

In order to know whether your child has the prerequisite reading skills for the assigned homework, you need to understand how reading prowess unfolds.

Reading levels progress this way:

Emergent reading: understanding what reading is, recognizing a few words

Early reading: being able to sound out words or string words together in short sentences

Con'-tent reading: getting information and plot from reading

Con-tent' reading: relaxed, accurate intake; fluency; use of punctuation for phrasing

Nimble reading: moving easily among factual, survey, and aesthetic reading

In grades 6-8, well-prepared students are comfortable at all these levels. Unfortunately, many students today received well-intentioned but inadequate early reading instruction. The malevolent harvest appears at these ages. Teachers don't feel responsible for giving reading instruction at these grade levels, yet students don't know what it is they don't know, and are stumbling along with bits and snatches of early skills. Ragged holes in their skills make booby traps in accuracy and comprehension. If reading is hard and doesn't make sense, intelligent kids avoid it. In order to read for meaning and enjoyment, your child needs the following prerequisites:

- The ability to recognize some words by sight

- The abilty to decode words (sound them out)

- The ability to encode words (spell them)

- The ability to transcode words (convert words and sentences into meaning)

Be sure your child's reading skills are solid. If you are concerned, request individual testing through the school system or get testing on your own. If your child is on or below grade level on standardized reading testing, get more information now. If there are holes in the skills, get help to plug them up now. Things will not get better on their own. Troubles will multiply and minor lapses turn into major catastrophes.

12. Do your child's developmental and language levels match the assigned tasks?

Academic tasks must match the learner's developmental level. In pithy, biting words, professor and linguist Anthony Bashir says that if we give children tasks beyond their developmental level, "they punish us by showing us how dumb they are."

Children reveal their developmental level by their humor and literary appetites. Most students in grades 6-8 are newly able to tolerate ambiguity. Holding competing ideas in their heads, they shuttle back and forth between them. For example, they accept that a character in a book may be a good person who does a bad thing, or identify with a character who is both loving and hurtful. Because this is a new ability, your child will enjoy exercising it. You can enhance this new capacity by providing opportunities in discussions of literature, TV shows, current events, or family dynamics.

You need to be on the lookout for the problem of "just because they could doesn't mean they should." Your child at this age is probably full of zany, conflicting, funny, and very serious ideas simultaneously. These are traits to encourage, refine, and channel. That doesn't mean stamp them out. Homework should open new ideas, new genres in writing and reading, new avenues for creativity. While it is possible to require a student in these years to produce a twenty-page research paper, the energy required will be out of proportion to what the student will learn.

If your child is caught in developmentally inappropriate assignments, talk to the teacher about the specific problem—see if there could be an option of doing two smaller papers instead of one giant one—or talk to the administrator of your child's division in school about the discontinuity between expectations and developmental levels as stated (one hopes) in the school's homework policy.

Understanding the combination of developmental appetites and language levels allows parents and teachers to coordinate homework and reading assignments with the child's natural interest levels and capacities. Bingo!

In the language domain, between grades 6-8, most children can make a concise definition: a sofa is a piece of furniture, a lake is a body of water, afraid is a bad feeling. Why do we care? The ability to make a definition represents the ability to sort out the most important facts from a whole collection of associations: I can sit on my sofa, but the dog isn't supposed to lie there; last week I dropped a piece of pizza, juicy side down, on the sofa and got in trouble; sofas are expensive.

The ability to sift and to retrieve what matters most (the salient feature) also underlies the ability to summarize and to think in hierarchies, and, thus, is prerequisite to higher learning, independent thinking, and, of course, homework. A child who cannot make a definition will struggle with the skills just mentioned.

Practice with your child. Start by giving an example, such as the one about the sofa. Talk about which facts are the most important and which one establishes the general category. Can your child define *pig, boat,* or *house?* Does your child establish the generic category? If not, use simpler examples, model the reasoning, and practice.

Children in junior high catch on to word derivations, understanding that words, like people, have ancestors, cousins, and offspring. To probe for this insight, you might start with the word *manual*, explaining that it comes from the Latin word *manus*, meaning hand. Brainstorm with your child other words that come from this same root and see if you can figure out what they mean. You will probably generate *manuscript*, script=writing, manus=hand, therefore *manuscript* means *handwriting* (see page 92).

Your child needs to be familiar with such linguistic devices as passive constructions, embedded clauses, dependent clauses, figures of speech, idioms, and similes.

If you say, "The girl was pushed by the boy," can your child tell who did the pushing?

If you say, "The girl, standing beside the man, was pushed by the boy," is your child sure whether it was the girl or the man who was pushed?

If you say, "That boy burned his bridges," does your child know what happened to the boy . . . and why?

If you say, "The girl, as delicate as a wildflower, was pushed by the boy," does your child think the girl was standing in a garden?

All of which is why I'll say, "Language, to be developed, needed by everyone, and the distinguishing mark of the human being, is a gem to be mined, common as excuses, and as exciting as a sunrise."

Your child and others in grades 6-8 are thrown into a game I call Lexical Leapfrog. All of a sudden, every subject matter has its own vocabulary or lexicon. The child in departmentalized learning moves from discipline to discipline, teacher to teacher, and lexicon to lexicon. For instance, your child may move from math (subtrahends and minuends) to language arts (predicates and homonyms) to Social Studies (serfs and vassals) to computer (Zip drive and Power Point) to art (perspective and luminescence) to athletics (defense and offense) to lunch (pizza and gross-outs) to free time (awesome and "like").

If your child has an innately strong language system, well and good. If this is a weak area, she may just get "languaged out." If this is likely to happen, help your child by writing the workaday vocabulary of each discipline on an index card for her to review before plunging into the concepts. Make vocabulary familiar through exposure and use, not through teaching lists. For difficult terminology, let your child draw to create a context and associations.

Language and developmental levels work together in supporting social/emotional growth and intellectual advancement. Using the comments above, be sure your child has the necessary foundations.

13. Do your child's handwriting skills match the task?

Yes, handwriting matters even in the electronic era. Encourage your child to choose either manuscript or cursive writing, and reward legibility. Ask your child to help you by writing out the shopping or errand lists that you dictate. Give a bonus for legibility. Give a double bonus for legibility and tidiness. This is an area where you can help without stepping on teachers' toes. Does handwriting matter? Emphatically yes. People need it for:

- Taking notes in the lecture after the battery on the laptop dies.

- Taking a phone message.

- Writing a thank-you letter. Kids deserve to know the life truth that people give better birthday presents to kids who write handwritten thank-you letters.

- Writing a love letter . . . and yes that day will come.

- Getting a job. A recent business publication ran an article titled "How to Nail Down That Really Great Job After the Interview." Suggestion #1: Write a handwritten letter of thanks to your interviewer!

In addition to handwriting, help your kid develop accurate keyboard fingering. The hunt and peck system slows down thought processes and breaks the connective rhythm between thoughts in the brain and words on the paper (or screen). If your child's school doesn't provide good keyboarding instruction, get it independently. Your child may object initially, but you can explain that it is just like exercises and warm-ups for athletics.

You can also teach your child rudimentary shorthand for high frequency words: b/c=because, w/o=without, hw=homework, ←=before, →=after. Let your child figure out symbols for high frequency terms in particular disciplines.

Remember that during these years, your child's mind will take huge leaps in terms of rate and volume of thought, ability to think in abstraction, and ability to enjoy conflicting ideas. These conceptual appetites deserve a willing, trained hand. When fingers and thoughts are out of sync, either the ideas are sacrificed on the altar of efficiency, or the appearance of the output suffers, leading teachers to give low marks.

14. Do your child's study skills and learning styles match the assigned tasks?

It is fair for you to hope that earlier skills are in place. Trust, but verify! Here are thirteen ways you can help your child build solid study skills:

1) Be sure the Time and Space Homework Pact is in good order. It assures organization.

2) Your child needs to be familiar with methods for note-taking, outlining, and highlighting (Look back at question 5).

3) Make sure your child is able to think in categories and arrange ideas in hierarchies. Without this skill, it is virtually impossible for independent study, i.e., homework, to be productive. (See question 12 on developmental and language levels).

4) Does your child understand and use the appropriate conventions for three different kinds of reading: factual, survey, and aesthetic? Factual reading must be accurate and is often nitpickingly slow. Survey reading requires the ability to skim and zoom in on vital information. Aesthetic reading requires imagery, the ability to lose oneself in a story, identifying with characters or periods of time, and to hear the music of the words. Often, simple recognition of these distinctions brings spontaneous improvement.

5) Children this age need a homework checklist of what's to be done and when each assignment is due. Ideally, the checklist will be in the front of his binder.

6) Be sure your child understands the vocabulary required for the assignment.

7) Use television with your child to develop and refine skills of summarizing and predicting.

8) Help your child activate prior knowledge; before setting out to learn new facts, bring to the forefront what he already knows about the topic.

9) Preview the text; skim the introduction, conclusion, questions, and glossary.

10) Use the five *wh-* words and one *h-* word for organizing thinking, as well as for reading and writing: *who, what, when, where, why, how.*

11) In conversation, in reviewing family activities, in choosing things to do, help your child practice the ability to compare and contrast.

12) Help your child put the main idea into his own words.

13) Teach your child to use the five Organizing Questions in approaching written work:

What do I already know?

What do I need to find out?

Where will I get my information?

How should I collate it?

What is my final product to be?

Asking and answering these questions ahead of time establishes such a skeletal structure that the actual work is nearly done before beginning it.

In addition to these concrete study skills, you need to understand your child's learning styles so you can measure the "goodness of fit" between how your child learns and what he is being asked to do. Just as each person has a unique and permanent fingerprint, each person has an individual learning style.

Learning styles show early, though of course children change and develop new skills as they mature. For this reason, it is silly to say of a twelve-year old, "Ellen is a visual learner." Pigeonholing is dangerous as well as foolish. Your child may show different styles and patterns in different settings and for different requirements. That said, I will also say from experience and from the research that dyslexia, learning disabilities, some kinds of giftedness (academic and other types), and proclivities send up their flags in school-age children. We need to be good interpreters.

Academic giftedness makes children chafe at pedantry, dullness, and repetition. These children need to be able to make connections between what they are learning in school, the outside world, and their imaginations. Potentially, homework is an ideal vehicle. Children who are gifted need time and opportunity to refine their talents as well as to trot in harness with their classmates. Homework can be a glorious opportunity.

Some children are both gifted and dyslexic or learning disabled. They have particular, but manageable, needs. Parents and educators need to help them in their areas of need and provide scope and exercise for talents. Unsupported weaknesses ache; unexercised talents itch. Parents need to budget time, money, and psychological and emotional resources accordingly, remembering that there is life after school, both now and in the long run.

Dreamers may need to sharpen up. Those who drift may be showing signs of ADD/ADHD (Attention Deficit Disorder/Attention Deficit with Hyperactivity Disorder). These terms are fashionable right now, and may be seriously overused. However, when the condition is real, it is really real. If you suspect this in your child, you may want to consult a neurologist or a psychiatrist.

Children who aren't gifted or learning disabled also possess different learning styles. For example, tempo varies widely among children this age. Some quick students zoom through concepts and work. Others like to spend lots of time on topics that interest them. Slower children may plod along, or, taking only a surface view, skim through and overlook important aspects.

Some learners like to receive small bits of information and then string those together into a concept. They are called sequential learners. Others need to see the big overall picture first, then they can break it down into its components, reassembling them into the whole. They are called simultaneous learners. These distinctions play a big role in children this age. Simultaneous learners may need to see an outline and illustrations of a concept first, or hear the names of the characters before trying to follow a plot. Trouble follows if a sequential learner has a freewheeling simultaneous teacher or a simultaneous student has a "one foot in front of the other" teacher.

When teaching style and learning style are markedly different, the resulting discomfort can be as intense as that of wearing an unlined jacket of Harris tweed over a new, deep sunburn.

15. What if your child has dyslexia or learning disabilities?

Many children who are good in math and science, who are skillful with their hands and show spatial awareness in their skill on the athletic field, in the art room, or in their ability to build and fix machinery, and who function particularly well in three-dimensional areas, may have weakness on the other side of the coin. These children sometimes struggle in the two-dimensional realms such as reading, writing, spelling, word problems in math, and organization of written work. Adults need to be aware of this discrepancy so as to recognize its legitimacy when it appears and then get appropriate help for the child.

Children who are weak, clumsy, or unenthusiastic readers by this age should be screened for dyslexia, a condition in which normal to above-average intelligence combines with difficulty in reading and writing. If dyslexia is present, the sooner it is caught the sooner remedies can go to work. Get a tutor if strong, frequent, and consistent help is not available within the school.

Children with diagnosed learning disabilities can learn when taught with appropriate methods and materials. The guiding principle is to break down the tasks into small, manageable bites.

As a parent, your job is to get a reliable diagnosis. Follow the prescription which grows from the diagnosis. Some schools offer excellent help right inside the system. If your child's school doesn't, you may have to consider moving or get outside help. This may be inconvenient and expensive but may, literally, save your child's life.

In the meantime, lobby for as many hands-on projects as possible, and know that, from time to time, you may need to read text materials aloud while your child is receiving the help that will open the doors to independent reading.

A good resource for information, literature, and conferences is The International Dyslexia Association (I.D.A.), 8600 LaSalle Rd., 382 Chester Building, Baltimore, MD 21286-2044, 410-296-0232.

16. Are your child's emotional habits and considerations taken into account?

The emotional climate of your child's homework time sets the stage for enjoyment and success or for discouragement and self-doubt. People of all ages develop emotional habits just as they learn physical habits. Through the experiences you orchestrate and your responses to your child's successes or failures, you play a huge role in the development of optimism and pessimism.

Erik Erikson, revered figure in the fields of psychoanalysis and human development, said that school-age children internalize the generalization "I am what I can make work." Children equate their worthiness (of parental love) with how they view themselves as students. Therefore, adults need to give them things they can make work.

My own work led me into the neuropsychological research on the limbic system, the emotional brain. This particular "mission control" has the power either to open or to close doorways and pathways to learning and memory. Frightened, embarrassed, humiliated and/or ashamed kids don't learn new information well. They also lose access to facts and information they already know. The emotional climate of the home and the classroom is in the hands of parents and teachers, and maintaining an atmosphere of trust, in which it is permissible to take a chance on an idea without fear of ridicule, is one of the most sacred trusts adults have.

Martin E.P. Seligman, author and professor of psychology at the University of Pennsylvania, demonstrates that children develop feelings of "learned helplessness" or "learned competence" depending on the outcome of their attempts. Those who tend toward learned helplessness cave in at the prospect of new or hard things and give up quickly in the face of discouragement. Those inclined to learned competence tackle challenges with gusto as though sipping from internal wells of lemonade. They know how to "walk like Mr. Jefferson," as we will see in the following story.

Sixth-grade students in an urban school were assigned a history project. They were to choose a character from a list of twenty historical figures, research the person's life, write a paper, and then make a few artifacts which that person might have used or admired. One child chose Thomas Jefferson. The child wrote the paper and then made three clay and paper artifacts. The first was a model of the tower and clock Jefferson designed for the field hands to see. It had only an hour hand because he thought that was enough information to read from a distance. Second, using a shoe box, the child made a model of the bed Jefferson designed for himself that opened on one side to his bedroom and on the other side to his library. Third was a fictional letter Jefferson might have dictated to John Adams on July 4th, the day they both died, trying to heal their rift. On the day of the presentation, this girl dressed as Mr. Jefferson to present her project. She said, "I learned a lot from this project and I really like knowing stuff. I think I know just how Mr. Jefferson would have walked. And now I can walk that way, too."

Your child can "walk like Mr. Jefferson," too. How?

First, the simple-sounding ideas in this book are the ingredients of satisfying work. Second, consciously acknowledge the role and power of emotions. They are not "extras." They are foundations.

Probably you know this intuitively; now you have scientific and clinical validation. Trust it.

Emotionally satisfying homework at this age helps both percolation and preparation. Jack Walsh, an eighth-grader in Washington, D.C., said, "Yes, I think homework is necessary. It's even a good idea. Just learning things in class isn't enough. You need to practice your methods at home. 'Specially in math. In history, you need to make comparisons. That takes time, and it's interesting. That's good homework."

A sixth-grade girl said, "I like good kinds of homework. It's fun to have time to mess around with things you like. For me, that's math and 'core' (in her school they combine English and history). You learn from practicing things you've already been taught. But if they give you things for homework that you're supposed to figure out on your own, you might figure it out a harder, longer, wronger way."

Parents often ask me how to build motivation. It's not hard. Motivation springs from confidence. Confidence is the natural flower of competence. Whether it is finding the sweet spot in tennis or learning how to spell a four-syllable word, be sure that your child is learning new competencies, and has opportunities to showcase and demonstrate them. You are an ideal audience. These bring confidence, which brings motivation.

There are four cultural factors we need to watch carefully for children this age, all of which have direct and indirect bearing on homework.

First, we seem to have a terror of tranquility. At lunch recently, in a hotel/restaurant/bar, four loudspeakers were simultaneously playing country western music, CNN headlines, a replay of a Dallas Cowboys game, and local weather and traffic. Eating, which can be a delicious opportunity for peace and quiet, became a four-way intersection for noise, data, distraction, and intrusion.

Second, we seem to have a fear of solitude. Children know how to enjoy their own company. Adults must be careful not to rob them of this nourishing capacity.

Third, surrendering to the militance of the multitaskers, we layer ourselves and our children in activities. Where does that leave cloud gazing and other activities which foster creativity and imagination?

Fourth, we have a reverence for the tidiness of answers over the messiness of questions. And yet it's easy to see what that does to originality and spontaneity.

These four, singly and together, fracture extended thought, steal the reflective time creativity requires, replace quiet with noise, and inject urgency into rumination. Yet independent thinking, which is to say homework, needs peace and quiet as well as purpose.

17. Do your child's memory skills match the requirements of the homework?

Memory's four main jobs are to:

- put things in

- file things as efficiently and as accurately as possible

- retrieve things as efficiently and accurately as possible

- use memories in combination with new things to make novel connections

The ability to lodge facts, emotions, concepts, and ideas in memory is enhanced by benevolent emotional climate, physical well-being (sufficient sleep, nourishment, and bodily comfort), and a "goodness of fit" between the developmental, language, and reading levels of the student and the materials. Let's consider two different kinds of memory, and then explore what you can do to help build your child's memory skills.

Short-term memory is just what the name implies: healthy people can remember what they did this morning, or an hour ago. Activities and information go in and stick for a short while. They are available for retrieval and for use.

Long-term memory is also what the name implies. Our minds and our brains transfer some items into long-term memory, available for retrieval, now and for decades to come. For example, I visited an Alzheimer's patient today. This man in his eighties is unable to remember the name of the person who has taken care of him for six months, but he can tell you every detail of the winning baseball game he pitched in college.

For students the trick lies in moving information from the short term into long-term storage. This requires time and is helped by a three-part glue. The glue recipe is:

1) Create an emotional climate in which intellectual/conceptual risk is safe.

2) Join hands-on physical experience with the event or information.

3) Attach language to the event or information.

In grades 6-8, the memory demands on your child might include remembering mathematical procedures, history facts, Spanish vocabulary, or literary plots. For children to remember what they have just read, they need to understand the reading as they go along. They cannot remember vocabulary or linguistic constructions beyond their reading level, and they cannot "remember" what hasn't gotten in to start with.

When your child has to memorize factual information, an acronym might help. For instance, I can remember the names of the five Great Lakes because of HOMES: Huron, Ontario, Michigan, Erie, and Superior. If your child needs to commit something to memory, encourage him to invent an acronym.

To lodge information securely in memory, three short practices are more effective than one long one.

Apart from homework, you can also offer your child practice in retrieving and combining. Exercising this kind of thinking pays big dividends in general cognitive development. An example might be, "How do you think tonight's basketball game was similar to last week's? How were they different? Has the team changed since last year?"

18. Does the homework attach new concepts to ones that are already familiar?

Students can't learn two unfamiliars at the same time. They need the "velcro" of the familiar as a place for new information to stick. To acquire new information in an orderly way, people need a supply of general information to act as the "familiar" onto which to hang what they are learning. For instance, a child with a concept of Thomas Jefferson will hang on to information about Monticello.

You can help in the following four ways:

First, help your child put experience into words. Language is one ingredient of the memory glue. This is an ideal way to introduce new vocabulary—by attaching it to the child's actual experiences.

Second, discuss current events: elections, sports, local events, and national figures so that these names and concepts are part of your child's conceptual equipment.

Third, use television as one of many sources of information. Used wisely, it can be more than cognitive anesthesia. For example, at the end of a program, have your child summarize the plot points and discuss the main idea.

Fourth, tell family stories. Be specific about where and when they happened, what life was like at that time. My grandchildren like to hear about my mother, a diminutive beauty who wore hats with veils and smoked cigarettes in long white holders. She carried a fur muff and went sledding in high-heeled boots.

In addition to being fun and weaving a rich tapestry of personal family associations, family stories provide historical context, vocabulary, imagery, emotional identification . . . all of which are the foundations of understanding literature and identifying with various eras in history.

You, as a parent, have the opportunity to bring family stories alive for your child. You are the one to bestow this gift that will be a treasure throughout your child's life and will be passed down to future generations. Do it.

19. Does your child's homework promote privacy, participation, and enjoying your kid?

Your child needs privacy in homework. Mistakes aren't shameful, but no one likes to make them in public. Even though your child at this age may be proclaiming independence, she still wants to please you. You can help by being forthright about the mistakes you make and by trying new things in front of and with your child.

Participation gives children a chance to share as much as they want about their current project or reading level, and gives the parent a chance to delight in burgeoning accomplishments without being nosy. When you are invited to participate, try to offer strategies and techniques rather than answers.

You can also participate by offering to chaperone a field trip or a game, or by working on make-up for the class play.

Perhaps the most important charter you have is to enjoy your kid. This vote of confidence, hard to codify but easy to spot, encourages pride, enjoyment, and energy.

20. Do you watch the "Plimsoll Line"? (No, it's not a new television show.)

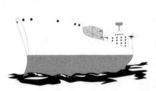

"The Plimsoll Line (sometimes called the Plimsoll Mark) is a circle with a horizontal line drawn through it, carried on both sides of all British merchant vessels. It indicates the maximum depth to which a vessel may be loaded, and is named after Samuel Plimsoll (1824-98) . . . who brought about its adoption in view of the great loss of life in overloaded vessels."

—*Brewer's Dictionary of Phrase and Fable*

Overloaded boats are in danger of wallowing or sinking, with possible loss of life. Could there be a better metaphor for homework? Think of your child as a boat with a hull, captain, crew, cargo, home port, and destination. The goal should be buoyancy, safety, and successful journeys.

Well-designed homework can be a time for reflection, tranquility, and solitude in people-packed days, an opportunity to think, wonder, question, and try new ideas. Harvard psychiatrist and author Edward Hallowell says:

"Remember that time of life when you were Lord of all the fields or Queen of all the stars and think now how much your capacity to dream and love and remember depends on your having had that once, that time when everything was new and lovely and possible and impossible all at once."

Keep your child's Plimsoll Line just where it belongs.

Bon voyage!

Priscilla L. Vail, M.A.T.

For more books and materials by Priscilla L. Vail, M.A.T., visit: http://www.priscillavail.com

Developing Good
Homework Habits

THE TIME AND SPACE HOMEWORK PACT—a "contract" between you and your child regarding where and when homework will be completed (see Introduction)—is the foundation on which success in schoolwork rests.

This chapter will discuss all the various details—such as time, location, and materials—necessary to make the Homework Pact effective. These details are like the fine print of a contract. However, before we get to all the small points, let's take a look at the Big Picture.

Location, Location, Location

As previously discussed in the Introduction, a good spot to do homework is one where your child can work without any major distractions.

> **A** good homework location should have adequate lighting as well as an area of flat space where your child can lay out some books and paper.

After you agree upon a location where your child will work, give him the opportunity to decorate it with posters, a corkboard with pictures of his friends, or other items that make him feel comfortable, but will not distract him from his homework for a long period of time.

Tools of the Trade

Following are lists of supplies that are helpful to have available in the homework location:

ESSENTIAL SCHOOL ITEMS

Pens (blue, black, and red)

Pencils

Paper (ruled and white)

Ruler

Dictionary

Simple calculator

Notebooks

Eraser

*T*o compute or not to compute? *Computer access at home is a nice convenience, but your child's education will not suffer if you don't own one. While students are often taught to use computers in school, there are no homework assignments that require your child to own a home computer. If your child needs access to a computer, many schools and local libraries have computer labs.*

Keep in mind that computers can also be a source of distraction. If your child has access to the Internet, she can easily spend several hours on the Web surfing instead of working. You may even want to check in on her occasionally to make sure that there is actual education afoot, and not some fast and furious video game.

NON-ESSENTIAL BUT HELPFUL ITEMS

Art supplies: glue, scissors, markers, poster-board

Math supplies: graph paper, compass, protractor

Term paper supplies: index cards, notebooks, a filing system of some sort

Computer supplies: computer paper, toner

USEFUL REFERENCE ITEMS

Thesaurus

Grammar book

Encyclopedia (CD-ROM version or regular)

Atlas

Certain projects may require additional supplies, which you can purchase on a case-by-case basis.

The reference items listed are definitely useful to have around, but don't tear your hair out if you don't have them. While it would be great to have access to an encyclopedia at your house, your child can get by just as easily by using the encyclopedias at the nearest branch library, or the ones at the school library, for that matter.

How To Help Your Child With Hard Facts

Often your child's homework assignments will involve quests for facts. For example, he may be asked to list all the state capitals. A good approach for this kind of assignment is to set up a series of steps your child should follow before asking for help from you. He should give every question his best shot, skipping over problems that are giving him trouble during his first pass through. Then he should spend some additional time trying to figure out the tough problems on his own, turning to reference books or other resources if necessary. If the extra time and other resources don't help, it's your turn to step in. When you do, remember:

•••••

Telling your child the right answer to a question is not as helpful as teaching him how to find the right answer to a question.

•••••

Working with your child on homework should give you an idea of your child's note-taking skills. If he says the answers to the homework assignment should be in his class notes and he is having a hard time finding them, the most likely reason is that your child is not taking enough (or correct) notes during class. Here's a good rule of thumb that your child should start to follow: If the teacher writes something on the board, make sure to write it down in your notes.

So if your child asks you to name the capital of Texas, try saying something like, "Let's think about it this way: what reference material could we use to find the answer to this question?" If your child says, "dictionary," have him check the dictionary. It turns out many dictionaries do list the capitals of states and countries, often near the back of the book in an index. If your child said "globe," "map," or "atlas," a quick survey of the proper map or atlas page would also yield the correct answer. Using this method, your child learns not only that Austin is the capital of Texas, but also that the capitals of states and countries can be found in an atlas, dictionary, or globe. This way, your child learns—and learns how to learn more in the future.

Another way to help your child on fact-based homework assignments is to encourage the use of *mnemonic* (pronounced "nuh-mon-ick") *devices*. Although a mnemonic device sounds like an expensive electronic gadget, it is in fact just a tool to help your child remember a certain fact. For example, let's say your child's assignment was to look up twenty vocabulary words and write down their definitions. This is a straightforward assignment, but the key is to understand the goal of the homework assignment. In this case, the goal is to learn the definitions of the twenty assigned words. If your child just writes down the definitions or doesn't understand a lick of what he's writing, he is going to have trouble when the time comes for him to define the vocabulary words on his own.

Not every word or fact lends itself to a mnemonic device. Some things will just have to be memorized. However, if you encourage your child to come up with mnemonic devices, it should help improve his memory, and it will make basic homework assignments designed to increase your child's base of knowledge more effective.

Here is where a mnemonic device comes in handy. Take the word *cacophony* as an example. You might ask your child to imagine a symphony where the musicians did nothing but cackle and cough the entire time. The words *cackle* and *cough* should remind him of the word *cacophony*. And a symphony of cackles and coughs would sound awful, wouldn't it? The dictionary definition of *cacophony* is "harsh or unpleasant sounds," and this easily describes a group of people making terrible noises. Instead of trying to remember a dry dictionary definition, your child can use the mnemonic device, visualizing the symphony of people cackling and coughing. This is much easier to remember, and when the time comes to define *cacophony* on a test, your child should be able to recall its meaning.

How To Help With Creative and Long-Term Assignments

An initial hands-off period works well for short, fact-intensive assignments like the vocabulary task described above. However, for longer, more involved homework assignments such as a five-page research paper, the opposite is true. Long, complex assignments benefit from proper planning and management of all the various steps needed to complete them, so sit down with your child before the project begins and help her plan out a good course of action. Once your child has a good idea of what she wants to write about, you can leave her to work on the project on her own. Here are some of the things you should discuss with your child when dealing with a research paper.

These points apply to most long-term projects. Long-term projects on a specific subject, such as a science experiment or creative writing assignment, will be covered in the subject-specific chapters later in this book.

Long-Term Project Planning Questions to Ask Your Child

1. In the most precise terms possible, what do you want the final project to be?

When asked to write a five-page paper about wildflowers, many students just start writing down every fact they can find about wildflowers until five pages are filled. Instead, help your child develop a precise main idea or topic sentence that she will then write about for five pages. "There are many types of wildflowers" is a very general statement and not likely to generate a good term paper. "Prairie wildflowers share many characteristics with wildflowers that grow only in the mountains" is a much more precise topic and will probably generate a better paper. In fact, with a precise statement your child can almost visualize what the rest of the paper will be. First, the characteristics of prairie flowers will be discussed, and then these will be compared with the characteristics of mountain flowers to show their similarities.

While this example deals with a research paper, having a clear goal works for most long-term projects. For example, your child can develop a precise focus for an art assignment that requires her to make a poster illustrating her favorite hobbies. "The poster will have something to do with sports" is not a very clear idea. To prompt her to clarify her idea, you could ask questions like, "Which sports will you include?" If she decides that softball is the only sport she will use, you could help her refine things even more by asking, "What part of softball do you enjoy the most? Is it hitting, pitching, or stealing home in the bottom of the ninth?" Depending on how she answers these questions, your child should be able to see her poster coming more and more into focus.

2. Now that you have a clear idea of what you want to accomplish, what are the steps you need to take?

The purpose of this question is to help your child break down a large project into a series of manageable tasks. It is difficult for most people to sit down and write 2,000 words about wildflowers from start to finish. It is much easier to write a single introductory paragraph, then a paragraph about prairie flowers, followed by a paragraph on mountain flowers, then a paragraph discussing their similarities, and so on. Talking about these steps should also help reveal all of the smaller sub-steps; for example, to write a paragraph about prairie flowers, your child must first do a little research on prairie flowers. To write a paragraph about mountain flowers, she needs to research mountain flowers. This leads to the inevitable step: go to the library.

By discussing and delineating the various stages needed to complete a project, you help your child transform a large, seemingly impossible assignment into a series of readily achievable steps. Breaking a project down into specific tasks also gives your child the flexibility to work on the small pieces of the project over a period of days before the finished product is due.

3. Will you need any special materials for any part of your project?

This question is closely related to question 2. Once your child has laid out all the various steps, she needs to decide what tools and supplies she will need to accomplish each stage of the project. If you do not have these materials around the home, then it is time to add another step to the project, called "Gather Necessary Materials."

On an assignment such as a research paper, the essential materials are probably just paper and pens (although your child might want to use index cards for organizing facts). However, there will have to be some research involved, so one step might be a trip to the local library. The question becomes, "What research materials will you need, and where can you find them?"

4. Roughly how long will each step of the project take?

All too often, students sit down the night before a ten-page research paper is due, only to realize there is no way they can complete the project without bending time and space.

If your child takes into account the time needed to finish each step before starting the project, she should be able to get a good idea of when she needs to start working on it. If possible, add time to the end of the project to give her some wiggle room, since you never know whether or not one section of the project is going to take longer than it should. Researching a topic often takes longer than students expect, simply because the information they are looking for is much harder to find than originally thought.

You now have a good method of approach for straightforward assignments as well as longer projects. Many assignments are a combination of these two extremes, but this is something you can work out with your child individually. If your child likes to attempt most assignments without your help at first, that's fine, as it promotes her personal educational development. If your child needs some encouragement before working, by all means give it to her.

Communicating With Your Child's Teacher

Up to now, we have been focusing on the importance of your role and your child's role in successful homework completion. As previously discussed, there is another person who plays an important homework role: your child's teacher. Establishing a good working relationship with your kid's teachers is vital. This does not mean that you should be calling the school every afternoon for a conference. Instead, the main goal between you and a teacher should be coordination. The better you understand what the teacher's goals are for your child, the better you will be able to help him when he does his homework in that subject.

What if You Get Stumped by Your Child's Homework?

It is bound to happen one day. Your child will ask you a question or show you a homework problem that you can't even understand, much less answer. There are two main reasons for this: first, it has been years since you were in junior high, and you just forgot a few things that are important for school work but not often used in everyday life. Second, the terms you used in school are not always the same ones your child is learning. For example, you wouldn't think a word like *subtract* would ever go out of style, but in some areas this word has been replaced by synonyms like *reduce* or *lessen*.

When faced with the inevitable stumper, don't worry. Remember, you may have forgotten a few things, but you are still much more experienced than your child at finding the information you need. You can turn the occasion into a learning experience for both you and your child as you track down the answer together.

Can You Make Homework an Enjoyable Experience?

o.

Truthfully, very few teenagers will enjoy doing homework. While you can't make homework something your child enjoys, you can help transform it into something your child does not fear, just something that needs to be done to learn the material. Your child may not smile too often while working on homework, but he can learn the material well with your help. The big smiles are reserved for when he takes the big test on the subject . . . and aces it.

This is when you'll both feel like Homework Heroes.

CHAPTER 2

A Review of Key Junior High Math Concepts

THE AMOUNT OF MATHEMATICAL KNOWL-EDGE your child will cover in his junior high school years will fill several large textbooks crammed with really small type. Don't worry. Following is a review of the four major concepts and ideas that are the lynchpins of math at this level: Number Sense and Numeration, Algebra, Geometry and Measurement, and Data Sense and Probability. If you refamiliarize yourself with these ideas, you should have the foundation you need to help with any junior high math homework.

Number Sense and Numeration

Quick! Think of three numbers.

If you are like most people, the first three numbers that pop into your head are 1, 2, and 3. This is a perfectly acceptable answer.

Now, think of three positive consecutive integers. Can you do it, or do any of these terms throw you for a loop? Read on.

Math Terms, Part I

Integers—Any whole number, which includes positive and negative numbers as well as zero. Basically, anything but a fraction or decimal is an integer.

Positive—Any number greater than zero.

Negative—Any number less than zero.

Zero—Neither positive nor negative.

Consecutive—Following one after the other in order. In math terms, this usually means going from least to greatest.

Having covered those terms, you can easily see that the numbers 1, 2, and 3 are a group of three consecutive positive integers.

Why do mathematicians insist on using terms like *integer,* when it seems that the word *number* would work just as well? Here are some possible reasons:

Reason A: Mathematicians enjoy confusing students, and then laughing about it at the monthly secret meeting of the Math Society.

Reason B: Mathematicians are aliens.

Reason C: Math is a very precise science, and you can't answer the question, "What is 7 minus 2?" with "Something around 1, I suppose." Similarly, the word *number* is not very precise: it could mean an integer (9), a mixed fraction (76½), a negative decimal number (-0.00056), or even an

To be honest, while Reason C is the correct answer, our personal favorite is B. It just explains so much!

irrational number (-6*i*). You need to be as precise as you can when discussing math, and to do that you need precise terms.

Number Lines and Absolute Values

The **number line** is a very useful, simple tool to help your child think about various math concepts. A basic number line looks like this:

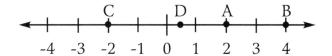

The number line has arrows on both ends to show that it continues in each direction endlessly, out to infinity. On this number line, you can see that A and C are both integers, although A is a **positive number** while C is a **negative number**. Looking at it drawn out this way, the concept seems very obvious. You can see that if you were to add B and C together, you would end up with a positive number, because B is farther to the right of zero than C is to the left of zero. Also, 4 − 2 = 2. A number line allows you to visualize this.

Math problems sometimes also deal with the **absolute value** of a number. Absolute value is the distance a number is from zero, regardless of whether the number is positive or negative. It is represented by putting a little vertical line on either side of the number, like this: |4| or |2|. Absolute value is always positive, unless the number in question is 0, in which case the absolute value is 0. So |-6| = 6 and |0| = 0 and |8| = 8.

Point D is between the integers 0 and 1, making it a fraction, our next topic of discussion.

Fractions

Most people can recognize a fraction when they see one, but it really helps to understand the idea of fractions completely. To do this, we will use pizza as an example. Seconds after the first pizza slice was created, this fraction explanation followed. (Please feel free to order pizza to help you both have dinner and follow along.)

EXAMPLE:

The pizza has been cut into eight slices, and the shaded piece is yours.

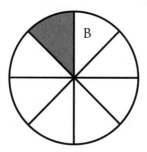

Fractions are used to describe a part of a whole. They are composed of two numbers: the bottom number is the **denominator**, and it shows the total number of pieces in the whole pizza. Since there are eight slices, the denominator is 8. The top number is the **numerator**, and it shows what part of the entire pizza is yours. Since you have one slice, the numerator is 1. Therefore, the fraction that describes your amount of pizza is ⅛.

$$\text{Fractions} = \frac{\text{Numerator}}{\text{Denominator}} = \frac{\text{Part of pizza}}{\text{Whole pizza}} = \frac{1}{8}$$

Let's give you another slice of the pizza, slice B. Does this change the denominator? The answer is no, since the total number of slices in the pizza remains eight. However, the part of the pizza that is yours does change, since you now have two slices. So the numerator

In general, when giving a fraction as a final answer, your child should use the simplest fraction possible, meaning reduce it to the lowest equivalent fraction. While $\frac{2}{8}$ is correct, it would be better to use $\frac{1}{4}$, since this is the simplest fraction.

becomes 2, and the fraction of the pizza you own is now $\frac{2}{8}$.

While $\frac{2}{8}$ is correct, you could also divide the numerator and denominator by 2 and get ¼ (this is called **reducing**). This is because ¼ and $\frac{2}{8}$ are **equivalent fractions,** meaning that they represent the same numerical value, even though their numerators and denominators are different. To visualize this on the pizza, imagine that your two slices suddenly became one really big slice and that the six remaining slices merged with each other in the same way. You still have the same amount of pizza, but instead of two smaller pieces out of eight smaller pieces, you have one bigger piece out of four.

Math Terms, Part II: Fractions

Equivalent Fraction—Fractions that are equal to each other. For example, $\frac{1}{2}$, $\frac{2}{4}$, $\frac{9}{18}$, and $\frac{345}{690}$ are all equivalent fractions.

Simple Fraction—A fraction whose numerator and denominator cannot be reduced to smaller numbers.

Mixed Number—A mixed number consists of a whole number and a fraction. Examples include 5 ½ and -6 ⅓. Mixed numbers can also be expressed as improper fractions.

Improper Fraction—A fraction where the numerator is greater than the denominator, as in $\frac{9}{4}$.

To convert an improper fraction to a mixed number, divide the numerator by the denominator. With the fraction $\frac{9}{4}$, 9 divided by 4 equals 2 with a remainder of 1, so the mixed number $2\frac{1}{4} = \frac{9}{4}$.

To change a mixed number like $4\frac{3}{5}$ into an improper fraction, first multiply the denominator (5) with the whole number (4), and then add the numerator (3) to this number. Since $5 \times 4 = 20$, and $20 + 3 = 23$, the improper fraction $\frac{23}{5} = 4\frac{3}{5}$.

Now it is time to add, subtract, multiply, and divide these fractions. Addition and subtraction are easiest, so we will start there.

To add or subtract fractions:

1) The denominators of both fractions must be the same.

2) If the denominators are not the same, find the lowest common denominator (see below) and create fractions that have the same denominator.

3) Once the denominators are the same, add (or subtract) the numerators only. The denominator stays the same for the answer.

4) If possible, reduce the answer to a simple fraction.

EXAMPLE:

$\frac{3}{8} + \frac{1}{8}$

If your child has to add $\frac{3}{8} + \frac{1}{8}$, he doesn't have to worry about the first two steps, since the denominator is 8 in both cases. $3 + 1 = 4$, so the answer is $\frac{4}{8}$, which can be reduced to $\frac{1}{2}$.

If the denominators are not the same, determine the **lowest common denominator,** which is the smallest number into which both denominators are divisible. Then restate the fractions in terms of the new common denominator.

EXAMPLE:

$\frac{1}{2} + \frac{1}{4}$

If your child has to add $\frac{1}{2} + \frac{1}{4}$, the solution is easy enough. The first step is to make the denominators of both fractions the same. We can quickly see that 4 is divisible by 2. So $\frac{1}{2}$ can be represented as $\frac{2}{4}$ (remember, both the numerator and the denominator must be multiplied by 2). Now, since both denominators are the same, all you have to do is add the numerators: ¾ + ¼ = ¾.

EXAMPLE:

⅞ + ½₂

Stumped on a Common Denominator?

If your child can't think of the least common denominator, he can always multiply the two denominators in the equation together to find a common denominator. He may wind up dealing with some pretty large numbers and have to reduce the fraction he gets as an answer quite a bit, but at least he will get the addition or subtraction right.

If your child has something a little more complicated, like ⅞ + ½₂, finding the lowest common denominator will be trickier. You need a number into which both 9 and 12 are divisible. In this case, 36 fits the bill (9 goes into 36 four times, and 12 goes into 36 three times). Since we are multiplying the denominator (9) four times, we have to do the same to the numerator (7). The fraction becomes ²⁸⁄₃₆. We increase the denominator (12) in the second fraction three times, so we have to do the same to that numerator (1). Our second fraction becomes ³⁄₃₆. Now we can add ²⁸⁄₃₆ + ³⁄₃₆ to get ³¹⁄₃₆ (which, by the way, cannot be reduced any further, so it is our final answer).

To multiply fractions:

To multiply fractions, you need only multiply the denominators together and the numerators together.

EXAMPLE:

⅘ × ⅜

Here, you simply multiply straight across and reduce. So let's take the numerators first:

$$4 \times 3 = 12$$

Now multiply the denominators:

$$5 \times 8 = 40$$

We now have the unreduced answer $\frac{12}{40}$. Since 4 can be divided into 12 and 40, we can reduce this fraction to $\frac{3}{10}$, our final answer.

To divide fractions:

1) To divide, you must first flip the fraction you're dividing by (the one after the division sign), so that the numerator becomes the denominator and the denominator becomes the numerator.

2) Then you multiply the two fractions.

EXAMPLE:

$$\frac{5}{6} \div \frac{2}{3}$$

First, flip $\frac{2}{3}$ to make it $\frac{3}{2}$. Now we have a multiplication problem we can handle just as we did earlier: $\frac{5}{6} \times \frac{3}{2}$. Multiply the numerators:

$$5 \times 3 = 15$$

Now the denominators:

$$6 \times 2 = 12$$

Here's a snappy little ditty to help your child remember how to divide fractions: When dividing, don't ask why, just flip it over and multiply!

The resulting unreduced fraction is $\frac{15}{12}$. This is an improper, unreduced fraction. To get our final answer, we should reduce first. The number 3 divides into the numerator and denominator, giving us a fraction of $\frac{5}{4}$. The number 4 goes into 5 once with a remainder of 1, leaving us with a final answer of $1\frac{1}{4}$.

Ratios, Percents, and Decimals

Ratios

Fractions are used to describe a part of a whole, and the definition of a ratio is very similar: ratios are a method used to describe a relationship between two numbers, or of a part to a part. Look back at the pizza slice example, on page 48. The fraction that describes your amount was ⅛. However, the ratio of your pizza to everyone else's pizza is 1:7, or one part of pizza for you to every seven parts of pizza to everyone else. When you received a second slice, the ratio would change to 2 parts for you and 6 slices remaining for everyone else, or 2:6.

Normally, a colon is used for ratios, like 2:6, but sometimes it is written like a fraction, such as 2/6. Watch out for this!

Often in everyday life, we find ourselves using ratios when cooking or making drinks.

EXAMPLE:

To make Grandma's Super-kicky Lime Punch, use one part lime juice to every three parts of water. How can the ratio of lime juice to water be represented?

Grandma's punch sure sounds tart, doesn't it? No wonder she always wears such a sour expression. Anyway, the ratio in her punch is 1:3. So if you had one measuring cup or one big spoon or one large trough, you would mix together one cup/spoon/trough of lime juice and three cups/spoons/troughs of water to make the punch. No matter what the unit of measure you use, the ratio remains the same.

Percents

The -*cent* in *percent* stands for one hundred, and it is easy to think of percent as meaning "out of a hundred." So 73% means 73 out of 100, and could be written as the fraction ⁷³/₁₀₀.

To convert a fraction into a percent, just—here comes some math lingo—convert that fraction into an equivalent fraction with 100 as the denominator, and then the numerator is your percent.

EXAMPLE:

Convert ¼ into a percent.

First, multiply both the numerator and the denominator by 25 to get a denominator of 100. The numerator of this fraction is the percent.

$(1 \times 25) = 25$ and $(4 \times 25) = 100$, so $^{25}\!/_{100} = 25\%$

Now try applying percentages to this problem:

EXAMPLE:

On a particularly sunny day in early spring, 10 students out of a class of 25 failed to show up. What percentage of the class was missing?

We know 10 out of 25 students did not come to class, so this means $^{10}\!/_{25}$ were out. To convert this into a percentage, we need to change our denominator to 100. In this particular case, that means multiplying both the numerator and denominator of this fraction by 4.

$10 \times 4 = 40$ and $25 \times 4 = 100$.

We are left with the fraction $^{40}\!/_{100}$, which is equal to 40%, our final answer (and quite a substantial rate of absenteeism).

Decimals

All numbers to the left of a decimal are for units greater than one, while everything to the right of a decimal is for units that are less than one. Since proper fractions are less than one, the relationship between fractions and decimals is fairly simple. A decimal number like 0.3 means three-tenths, and you can write it $^{3}\!/_{10}$. If your decimal number extends to the thousandths place, like 0.343, then you would place 343 over 1000, as in $^{343}\!/_{1000}$. Think of it this way:

•••••

However many spaces a decimal number extends to the right,
that's how many zeroes you place after a "1" in the denominator.

•••••

To convert a fraction into a decimal, just divide the numerator by the denominator. This doesn't always work very neatly. You may find yourself with a very long decimal number, or even one that goes on in the same repeating pattern to infinity. A decimal that repeats the same pattern to infinity is a **repeating decimal**; for example, $\frac{4}{11}$ equals 0.36363636 . . . (which is also represented as $0.\overline{36}$). A long decimal number that never shows a repeating pattern and goes on to infinity is a **nonrepeating, nonterminating decimal**. So the fraction $\frac{22}{7}$ equals 3.142857143 . . . and on and on without repeating. Your child can usually just round these off after three or four decimal places, depending on the teacher's preference.

To switch between a percent and a decimal, just multiply the decimal by 100 to get the percent. Therefore, 0.56 becomes 56%, while 0.2 becomes $0.2 \times 100 = 20\%$.

Homework Heroics: Units of Measure and Good Old American Stubbornness

EVEN THOUGH ALMOST all of the rest of the world uses the metric system, where everything is divisible by ten, we steadfastly stick with the hodge-podge of measurements the British gave us. Luckily, converting back and forth from metric to British—and just converting between different units of measure—is great word problem practice. Your child can have fun converting measurements she sees every day, like miles per hour or pounds, into metric measurements, or doing things like figuring out how many cups of water are in her twenty-gallon fish tank, or how many feet are between one town and the next town.

Exponents and Scientific Notation

Exponents

To understand the need for these concepts, your child should think about this mantra: Mathematicians are lazy! You see, they don't want to waste time writing out something like $5 \times 5 \times 5 \times 5 \times 5$, so they created the exponent, which transforms $5 \times 5 \times 5 \times 5 \times 5$ into 5^5, which is read "five to the fifth power." The small, raised number is called the **exponent**, and it indicates the number of times the base number is multiplied by itself. The exponent in 2^3 tells you to multiply the number 2 three times, or $2 \times 2 \times 2$, read as "two to the third power."

Squares and Cubes—It turns out that 2 and 3 are favorite exponents, so they have their own special "nickname" way of being read. For instance, 4^2 is most commonly read "four squared" and 4^3 is read "four cubed." You can say "to the second power" or "to the third power" and still be correct, but "squared" and "cubed" are what all the really cool mathematicians say.

EXAMPLE:

$2^6 =$

Working with exponents is fairly easy, but a little cumbersome. To tackle these problems, just write out the numbers and do your multiplication:

$$2^6 = 2 \times 2 \times 2 \times 2 \times 2 \times 2 = 64$$

Your child may even be faced with a negative exponent. Not to worry! All she needs to do is:

1) Remove the negative sign.

2) Work the exponent out using multiplication.

3 Then drop the result under the number 1 and make it the denominator in a fraction.

EXAMPLE:

$4^{-3} =$

Start by treating it like a positive exponent.

$4 \times 4 \times 4 = 64$

Then just put your answer under 1. So the final answer is $\frac{1}{64}$.
Here's one last tip:

$$X^1 = X \text{ and } X^0 = 1$$

That means $4^1 = 4$ and $4^0 = 1$, or $129^1 = 129$ and $129^0 = 1$.

Adding, Subtracting, Multiplying and Dividing with Exponents— To add and subtract with exponents, you must simplify the numbers first, then perform the operation. This holds true whether the base numbers are the same or different.

To multiply exponents that have the same base, keep the base and add the exponents. So: $2^4 \times 2^6 = 2^{10}$. To divide exponents that have the same base, keep the base and subtract the second exponent from the first. So: $2^{10} \div 2^6 = 2^4$. If the bases are different, there's no easy way to deal with it. You must simplify each number and then perform the operation.

Scientific Notation

Mathematicians, hoping to save even more time (so they could take long lunches and sneak out of the office a little early on Friday), also created scientific notation. This is a way of taking a number with a lot of zeroes in it and reducing it so that there is not as much writing.

A number written in scientific notation looks like 3.65×10^7. It literally means $3.65 \times 10 \times 10 \times 10 \times 10 \times 10 \times 10 \times 10 = 36,500,000$. However, the clever thing about scientific notation is that, to expand the number to its correct figure, you need only move the decimal place the value of the exponent, which in this example is 7. So take the decimal between the 3 and the 6 and move it seven places to the right, adding zeroes for a place-holder if you need to. Ta da! You will get 36,500,000.

You try one:

EXAMPLE:

$4.78 \times 10^{12} =$

To tackle this, just scoot that decimal between the 4 and the 7 to the right 12 spaces, so your final answer is:

$$4.780000000000,00000$$

Scientific notation can also be used on very small numbers, like 0.000000053. In this case, the exponent will be negative, as in 5.3×10^{-8}, showing that you must move the decimal point 8 places to the left for this number.

·····

Negative exponents = move decimal to the left.

Positive exponents = move decimal to the right.

·····

Roots

Roots are like the flip side of exponents. The **square root** of a number is the number that, when multiplied by itself, gives you the original number. The **cube root** of a number is the number that, when multiplied by itself three times, gives you the original number. The symbol for a square root is $\sqrt{}$ and the symbol for a cube root is $\sqrt[3]{}$. All this is easier shown than defined, so look at these examples of common roots.

SOME COMMON SQUARE ROOTS

$\sqrt{0} = 0$ $\qquad$ $\sqrt{1} = 1$ $\qquad$ $\sqrt{4} = 2$ $\qquad$ $\sqrt{9} = 3$

Numbers that are perfect squares, or multiples of a perfect square, can be taken out from a square root and simplified. Perfect squares are numbers such as 9 (3^2), 16 (4^2), 25 (5^2), and so forth. In this way $\sqrt{25} = 5$. A number like 75 is a multiple of a perfect square, so it can be simplified in the following way:
$\sqrt{75} = \sqrt{25} \times \sqrt{3} = 5\sqrt{3}$.

$\sqrt{16} = 4 \qquad \sqrt{25} = 5 \qquad \sqrt{36} = 6$

$\sqrt{49} = 7 \qquad \sqrt{64} = 8 \qquad \sqrt{81} = 9$

$\sqrt{100} = 10$

A FEW CUBE ROOTS

$\sqrt[3]{8} = 2 \qquad \sqrt[3]{27} = 3 \qquad \sqrt[3]{64} = 4$

The square root of 25 is 5 because 5 × 5 equals 25. The square root of 49 is 7 because 7 × 7 equals 49. The cube root of 64 is 4 because 4 × 4 × 4 equals 64.

Luckily, since the advent of calculators, most students are spared having to work out more complicated roots by hand. Sometimes your child will be asked to approximate a square root, however. See the example below:

EXAMPLE:

Approximate $\sqrt{30}$.

To tackle this, think about what you already know. You know the square root of 25 is 5 and the square root of 36 is 6. This must mean that the square root of 30 is somewhere in between 5 and 6. Experiment by multiplying a couple of numbers close to 5.5 together, and then list your best approximation (probably something like 5.4).

Order of Operations

The Order of Operations determines what order you have to follow when doing arithmetic. It goes like

(Parentheses, Exponents) (Multiplication, Division) (Addition, Subtraction), a.k.a. PEMDAS.

EXAMPLE:

$$(2 + 3) - 3 \times 25 + 8 \div 2 =$$

First, you have to work anything within parentheses or that has exponents, leaving you with

$$5 - 3 \times 25 + 8 \div 2 =$$

Multiplication and division are done next. 3 and 25 are multiplied and 8 is divided by 2.

$$5 - 75 + 4 =$$

Save the addition and subtraction for last.

$$5 - 75 + 4 = \text{-}66.$$

A good way to remember the order of operations, PEMDAS, is with the phrase "Please Excuse My Dear Aunt Sally." Of course, if you have a sister named Sally who is very sensitive to criticism, feel free to change the name to Sue.

Algebra

Do you remember when you were a small child, and as such, were in a state of continual mock warfare with other kids in your neighborhood? Think back to the time you and your friends were planning the grand assault on your enemies' fortress. (Depending on where you grew up, this fortress might have been a treehouse, equipment shed, sand castle, igloo, or abandoned 1957 Chevy.)

There you were, drawing up plans in the dirt. Of course, you didn't have an actual exact figurine of the enemy stronghold, so you just used a large rock instead. The large rock stood for the enemy fortress, everyone understood that, and plans for the attack could move ahead accordingly.

The basic essence of algebra is all about using that big rock and making it stand for something else. In math terms, if you don't know the precise value of a number, you substitute a **variable** (think rock), which is a symbol that stands for an unknown quantity, in its place

When a number is being multiplied by a variable, the multiplication sign is commonly dropped. Therefore, 40 × y or 40(y) will be written as 40y. Division, addition, and subtraction signs are always used.

until its real value can be determined. This variable is usually a letter of the alphabet, written in italics (you most often see x or y).

Key Algebra Terms

Commutative Property—Addition and multiplication are commutative, because it doesn't matter in which order you add two numbers, or multiply two numbers, the answer will still be the same. Subtraction and division are not commutative. So 4 + 2 is the same as 2 + 4, since the answer in each case is 6, but 5 − 3 is not the same as 3 − 5, because in the first equation the answer is 2, while in the second equation it is -2.

Associative Property—When an operation appears twice in an equation, if it doesn't matter how you group the terms, it is said to be associative. Addition and multiplication are associative; subtraction and division are not. (4 × 2)5 is the same as 4(2 × 5), since they both equal 40, but (12 ÷ 3) ÷ 4 equals 1, so it is not the same as 12 ÷ (3 ÷ 4), which equals 16.

Distributive Property—This property governs how to "distribute" the number on the outside of a set of parentheses to the numbers inside. You can only use this when two functions are involved. So 4(5 + 12) = 4(5) + 4(12). You get the same answer because multiplication is distributive over addition. Addition is not distributive over multiplication, since 4 + (5 × 12) does not equal (4 + 5) (4 + 12).

Identity Element—The identity element for any function is the number that leaves other elements in the operation unchanged. For addition, this is 0, since any number plus 0 is that number. For multiplication, the identity element is 1.

Performing an inverse operation is a way to cancel out or "undo" another operation. The inverse of a number is 1 divided by the number, so the inverse of 5 is $\frac{1}{5}$. This process is used most frequently to eliminate a fraction in an equation with a variable.

Additive Inverse Element—This is the number that gives you 0 when adding. The additive inverse of 3, for example, is -3, since $3 + -3 = 0$.

Multiplicative Inverse Element—This is the number that gives you 1 when multiplying. The multiplicative inverse of 3 is $\frac{1}{3}$, since $3 \times \frac{1}{3} = 1$.

Simple algebra problems provide your child with the equation, and all he has to do is find the exact value of the variable. Harder questions require your child to set up the equation himself and then solve it.

EXAMPLE:

$5h + 23 = \frac{2h}{3} - 9$. Solve for h.

First, before isolating the variable, all elements are multiplied by 3 to eliminate the fraction $\frac{2h}{3}$ (this is called an inverse operation).

$$5h \times 3 + 23 \times 3 = \frac{2h}{3} \times 3 - 9 \times 3$$
$$15h + 69 = 2h - 27$$

At this point, you should work to isolate the variable h on one side of the equation, and bring all the numerical values over to the other side.

$$15h - 2h + 69 = 2h - 2h - 27$$
$$13h + 69 = -27$$
$$13h + 69 - 69 = -27 - 69$$
$$13h = -96$$
$$\frac{13h}{13} = \frac{-96}{13}$$
$$h = -7\,\frac{5}{13}$$

While this problem has many steps, all you have to do is write down all the work and do the arithmetic properly. The next one requires you to think up the equation yourself.

EXAMPLE:

You are the accountant for a local sporting goods store. Your store sells three different types of backpacks. The deluxe backpack costs $145, the medium-range backpack costs $92, while the economy backpack costs $45. Let t represent the total amount of money made on backpack sales for the store last year. If d represents the number of deluxe backpacks sold, m represents the number of medium backpacks sold, and e represents the number of economy backpacks sold, then what algebraic equation represents the money received last year on backpack sales?

This example is a little involved, and if your child tried to work out the problem in his head, he could easily get the facts confused.

•••••

Encourage your child not to work algebra problems out in his head. The more he writes down, the better his chances are of solving the problem correctly.

•••••

For this example, write out which variable represents each type of backpack:

d = number of deluxe backpacks sold

m = number of medium range backpacks sold

e = number of economy backpacks sold

t = total amount of money made on backpack sales

Now, if each deluxe backpack costs $145, you can figure out how much money the store made on deluxe backpacks. You should come up with $145 $\times$ d, the cost of each deluxe backpack ($145) multiplied by the number of backpacks sold d. This would be simplified to $145d$.

Do the same for the other two backpacks. Now, to find the total cost, you need to decide whether to add, subtract, multiply, or divide the three terms. The answer is add, since that's how to find the total amount of money. This gives you the answer: $t = 145d + 92m + 45e$.

Shouldn't answers be actual numbers like 2 or 44? Alas, in algebra this is not always the case. Sometimes the key is to find the precise numerical value of a variable, but other times the key is just to see whether or not your child can use algebra—and variables—correctly to set up the proper algebraic expression, like $t = 145d + 92m + 45e$.

Let's try one more example, a classic word problem involving trains, time, speed, distance, and rates.

EXAMPLE:

A nonstop train called the Texan Zephyr leaves Austin heading for Houston at 3:30 P.M. traveling at a constant rate of 30 miles per hour. Another nonstop train, called the Lone Star Express, leaves Austin at 4:00 P.M. traveling at a constant rate of 50 miles per hour. The Lone Star Express reaches Houston at 7 P.M. When does the Texan Zephyr arrive in Houston?

To solve this, you have to figure out how many miles there are between Austin and Houston. Luckily, the clues are in the problem. The Express travels from 4 P.M. to 7 P.M. at a rate of 50 mph. So:

3 hours × 50 mph = 150 miles from Austin to Houston

Let's apply this knowledge to the Zephyr part of the problem. The Zephyr leaves Austin at 3:30 P.M. We need to know how long it will

---

Homework Heroics: Real Life Algebra

IF YOUR CHILD wants extra help setting up algebraic equations, you can always quiz him with real-life scenarios to help him get better. Take football, for example. To figure out how many points a team scored, the equation you could use for most games is $s = 7t + 3f$, where s= total score for one team, t = touchdowns scored, and f = field goals made. For extra practice, see if your child can modify the equation, since a touchdown is really only worth 6 points, with an extra point or two-point conversion to follow.

take a train traveling 30 mph to go 150 miles. We might set up our equation this way:

$$x \text{ hours} \times 30 \text{ mph} = 150 \text{ miles}$$

Divide both sides by 30 to isolate x. We are left with the answer 5. That means the Zephyr will take 5 hours to reach Houston. Add 5 hours to 3:30 P.M., and you get your final answer: 8:30 P.M.

Polynomials and Monomials

A **monomial** is an algebraic expression that has only one term, like $10y$, $5q$, or $93s$. A **polynomial** has more that one term, like $6y - 10z$ or $7f + ysd + 64u$.

Adding and Subtracting Monomials

Follow the same rules you do with numbers as long as the terms are alike. So $10x - 3x = 7x$ and $15ys + 2ys = 17ys$. (Notice that the variables stay the same.)

Adding and Subtracting Polynomials

Line up the like terms and perform the operation. So:

$$
\begin{array}{r}
5a^2 + 4xy + 7q^3 \\
- (2a^2 + xy + 3q^3) \\
\hline
3a^2 + 3\,xy + 4q^3
\end{array}
$$

Multiplying and Dividing Monomials

Just apply the rules used for exponents (see pages 56-57) to the variables. So:

$$x^3 \times s^4x^2 = s^4x^5$$
$$q^4u^8 \times q^5u^2 = q^9u^{10}$$
$$q^8 \div q^7 = q$$
$$ys^5 \div y^3s = y^{-2}s^4$$

Multiplying Polynomials—Multiply each term in one polynomial by each term in the other, then simplify. With a binomial (the most complicated polynomial your child will face at this stage), use the **F.O.I.L. method**: multiply the First terms together, the the Outside terms, then the Inside terms, the the Last terms. Then simplify.

Here is an example:

$$(2x + b)\ (3x - 3b)\ = 6x^2 - 6xb + 3xb - 3b^2$$
$$= 6x^2 - 3xb - 3b^2$$
$$= 3(2x^2 - xb - b^2)$$

Dividing Polynomials—Make sure both polynomials are in descending order (the powers of the terms decrease from left to right), then do long division.

Functions

Functions are relations in which every value of x has only one value of y. Functions are very similar to algebra, and working with them usually just requires your child to follow directions. They look like:

EXAMPLE:

The function $f(x)$ is defined as $f(x) = 14r - 8b$. What is the value of $f(x)$ when $r = 2$ and $b = 4$?

If you think the way to solve this is to simply replace r with 2 and b with 4 in the original expression, and then just do the math, you're exactly right. $f(x) = 14r - 8b = 14 \times 2 - 8 \times 4 = 28 - 32 = -4$.

Geometry and Measurement

There are approximately forty-three bajillion rules and formulas concerning geometry (since geometry and measurement are so closely related, this book will talk about both subjects under the single term *geometry*). We will cover many of the big rules here, but it's a good idea to have a reference sheet somewhere in case your child forgets how to find the area of a triangle. Because we're the kind of folks who believe in convenience, we decided to provide a short reference sheet for you here. Bear in mind that these are just a few of the many formulas your child may be asked to use in geometry class.

FORMULAS FOR COMMON GEOMETRICAL SHAPES

Shape	Perimeter	Area	Volume of Solid
Circle	$2\pi \times \text{radius}$	$\pi \times \text{radius}^2$	
Rectangle	2(length+width)	length × width	length × width × height
Triangle	side+side+side	½base × height	
Parallelogram	side+side+side+side	base × height	
Trapezoid	side+side+side+side	½height(base1 +base2)	
Cylinder			$(\pi \times \text{radius}^2)\text{height}$

Circles

Let's begin our geometry discussion with one of the simplest geometric shapes, the circle.

While both you and your child could probably pick a circle out of a police lineup, it is a good idea to be able to define it. A **circle** is a two-dimensional shape in which every point along its edge is the same distance from the center. The circle above has its center at O, and all the points along its edge are the same distance from the center. So **line segment** OB equals OA, and both of these are equal to OC. If you were to draw in line segment OE, then it would be equal, also.

Now the linear distance from the center of a circle to its edge is called a **radius**, and OB is an example. A line running from one edge of a circle while passing through the center—such as line segment AC—is called the **diameter**. Since this line consists of AO and OC joined together, and since AO and OC are both **radii**, then *the diameter of a circle is always twice its radius.* A **chord** is any line whose endpoints are on the perimeter of the circle, but a chord doesn't have to pass through the center.

Now suppose that the circle currently under discussion was made out of string. If you were to pick up that string and place it next to a ruler, you would learn the distance around that circle, or the length of the circle's outer boundary. This distance is known as the **circumference** of the circle. Before you start cutting string to place around the circle in order to find its circumference, here are two handy formulas:

Circumference of any circle = 2 × (radius) × π, or $C = 2\pi r$
Since the diameter of a circle is twice the radius, this can also be written $C = \pi d$.

Where did this π (**pi**) come from? Well, I'll tell you a story. A long time ago, mathematicians figured out that every time they drew a circle, regardless of its size, and then divided that circle's circumference by its diameter, they came up with the same number, which they called pi. Since

Circumference ÷ Diameter = π, or $C \div d = \pi$, if you multiply d to both sides of this equation you get
$C = \pi d$, or $C = 2\pi r$.

Because the value of pi never changes, it is known as a **mathematical constant**. A rough estimate of pi is about 3.14159, although, in fact, the decimal units go on and on and the exact value of pi has never been determined.

While the circumference of the circle is the distance around its edge, the area of a circle is all the space inside. Once again, pi is used in the formula.

Area = π × radius × radius, or A = πr². (Return of the exponent! See pages 56-57.)

Before we move on to other topics, we need to clear up a couple of terms that get bandied about no matter what geometrical shape is being discussed: similar and congruent. These are easy to keep straight:

•••••

Similar figures are alike in shape and proportion, but not size.
Congruent figures are exactly the same size and shape.

•••••

Lines

The circle is a nice curvy little guy, but most basic geometric shapes are created by lines.

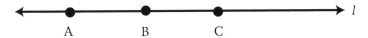

The arrows at the ends of line *l* illustrate that line *l* goes on forever in each direction, so there's no way to measure the distance of line *l*. However, you can measure line segments, such as AB, BC, and AC. If AB = 3 and BC = 4, you can easily work out that AC = 7.

Time to spice things up by adding more lines!

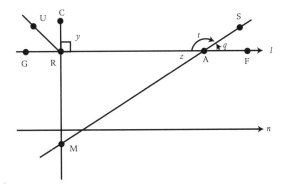

ngle q on page 69 can also be written as ∠SAF, since ∠SAF describes the intersection that creates the angle. Also, while most lines eventually will intersect, parallel lines never do; they are always the same distance apart. In this example, lines l and n are parallel, and this is written l ∥ n.

Okay, with this figure we have a number of things to talk about besides line segments. The **intersection** of two lines is the place where they cross. The intersection creates an angle, such as q.

Angles come in several different sizes, all of which are based primarily on the idea that a complete circle is 360 degrees, (or 360°). So, if you take a line—like the diameter—and cut a circle in half, how many degrees would you have? $360 \div 2 = 180$, so a line measures 180°.

Looking at this means that $t + q = 180°$. If you found out that $q = 30°$, you could now find the exact value of t (150°).

Common Angle Terms	Examples
Right angle—any angle that equals 90°.	∠GRC, ∠MRA, y
Acute angle—any angle that measures from 0° to less than 90°.	q, ∠MAR
Obtuse angle—any angle greater than 90° but less than 180°.	∠MAF, t
Supplementary angles—a pair of angles that add up to 180° (straight line).	t and q
Complementary angles—two angles which add up to 90° (right angle).	∠GRU and ∠URC
Vertical angles—two angles lying on opposite sides of two intersecting lines. Vertical angles are always equal.	q and z

If you took a line and divided it in half by drawing another line right through the middle of it, how many degrees would you have? The answer is 90°, and the angle that it creates is commonly referred to as a **right angle**; the two lines that meet at a right angle are called **perpendicular lines**. Angle y is a right angle, and it is denoted by the upside-down L thingee coming from angle CRA. Much of geometry focuses on right angles, so be prepared to see that symbol a lot.

Once your child familiarizes himself with these concepts, many geometry questions then become a matter of finding out one value, and then using all these various rules to determine the other values.

Triangles

Three intersecting lines form a **triangle**, a very common geometric shape.

Triangles have all sorts of cool rules about them. Here are the two most useful ones:

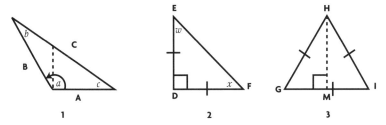

1. In every triangle, the sum of the three interior angles is always equal to 180 degrees.

In Triangle 1, since angle a is obtuse (greater than 90°), you know that $b + c$ must be less than 90°, otherwise the sum of all three angles would be greater than 180°. That's bad! In fact, if the figure has more than 180°, it is not worthy of the name *triangle* at all.

In Triangle 2, sides ED and DF are the same length, or congruent, to each other. A triangle with two equal sides is known as an **isosceles triangle.**

2. If two sides of a triangle are equal to each other, then the angles opposite those sides are also equal.

Using this knowledge, we can tackle the following problem:

EXAMPLE:

What are the measurements of the angles in Triangle 2?

Since ED = DF, then angle DEF = angle DFE, or $w = x$. Looking at the third angle, you can see a right angle signifier, so at this point you can do a little algebra to figure out all the angles of this triangle.

180 = sum of three sides of a triangle
180 = 90 (angle EDF) + $w + x$
Isolate the variable by subtracting 90 from both sides.
$90 = w + x$
Since $w = x$ you can also write
$90 = 2w$ or $90 = 2x$
Divide both sides by 2 and you get
w = 45°, so x also equals 45°.

*T*he dashes in ED and DF (on page 71) are used to show congruency without explicitly writing ED = DF. This is similar to brushing your finger along your upper lip as a way of telling someone they have bread crumbs there—it means the same thing, but you don't state it out loud.

Using only two dashes and a right angle symbol, you were able to discover the value of all three angles.

As you can see, Triangle 3 has three dash marks, meaning all three sides are equal. This is called an **equilateral triangle**. (A triangle so ill-mannered as to have no equal sides is called a **scalene triangle**.) Using the steps above, you should be able to figure out that each angle equals 60°.

Area and Perimeter of a Triangle

To find the perimeter of a triangle, simply add up its sides. There's nothing very exciting about that, although you can see that since all three sides of an equilateral triangle are the same, then the perimeter for this triangle equals three times the length of one side, or P = 3s.

Remember the formula for the area of a triangle on page 67? No? Here is it again:

Area of triangle = ½ × base × height , or A= ½ bh.

The values you use to find area can vary depending on which side of the triangle is the base. Whichever base you use, the height has to be measured at a right angle to this base. On Triangle 2 this is easy to do, since it contains a right angle. If you use DF as the base, then DE would be the height. If DE is the base, then DF becomes the height, but it doesn't really matter since you are multiplying the same numbers together in each case. On Triangle 3, however, if GI is your base, then the height must be found by measuring HM.

The Pythagorean Theorem

But how can HM be measured? The answer to this question lies in the **Pythagorean Theorem**, named after the Greek mathematician Pythagoras, which is usually stated like this:

$A^2 + B^2 = C^2$, where C is the hypotenuse.

The Pythagorean Theorem works only with right triangles. In a triangle like this—we'll use Triangle 2 for our example, but you can see that GMH in Triangle 3 is also a right triangle—the side opposite the right angle is called the **hypotenuse**. If you square the measure of the hypotenuse, you will find it equal to the sum of the squares of the other two sides.

EXAMPLE:

In Triangle 2 (page 71), what is the length of EF?

In Triangle 2 this means

$ED^2 + DF^2 = EF^2$

So if ED = 3 and DF = 4, then to find EF you would use

$3^2 + 4^2 = EF^2$

$9 + 16 = EF^2.$

$25 = EF^2$ or $5 = EF$

EXAMPLE:

What is the area of Triangle 3 (page 71) if HI = 6?

On Triangle 3, if you knew only one side of the triangle, you could find the area. You just need to do some fancy Pythagorean footwork to find out the height. For example, if HI = 6, then you know that each of the three sides equals 6, so GH = 6. The height HM cuts GI in two, so GM = 6 ÷ 2 = 3. Pythagoras says that

$GH^2 = GM^2 + HM^2$

You know the values of GH and GM, so you could find HM.

$6^2 = 3^2 + HM^2$

$36 = 9 + HM^2$

$36 - 9 = 9 - 9 + HM^2$

$27 = HM^2$

$\sqrt{27} = HM$

Once you do that, you just plug those values into the area of a triangle formula, A= ½ bh.

$A = ½(6 \times \sqrt{27})$

$A = 3\sqrt{27}$

Simplifying $\sqrt{27}$, we get $3\sqrt{3}$, and $3(3\sqrt{3})$ is $9\sqrt{3}$ square units, our final answer. (See simplifying square roots, p. 59).

Quadrilaterals

Shapes made out of four lines are all **quadrilaterals**, which literally means "four-sided," but there are some special cases that are known by different names.

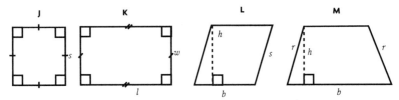

Squares and Rectangles—If you take four lines of equal length, make the opposite lines parallel to each other, and make all of the interior angles right angles, then you have a **square.** Figure J is a square, but don't say that to its face, OK? Figure K is a **rectangle,** which is similar to a square except not all four sides are of equal length. Opposite sides are equal to each other, though.

Rhombuses, Trapezoids, and Parallelograms—Figure L is a quadrilateral that has four equal sides, and opposite lines are parallel to each other, but the interior angles are not right angles. This is called a **rhombus.** Figure M is a **trapezoid,** a shape with one set of lines parallel to each other. The area and perimeter formulas for most of these figures are listed in the chart on page 67.

A **parallelogram** is a quadrilateral in which opposite sides are parallel. (A rhombus is a type of parallelogram.)

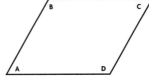

Some parallelograms can have angles that do not measure 90°. Luckily, there are a couple of convenient rules you can use when dealing with the angles of a parallelogram:

1)   Opposite inside angles of a parallelogram are congruent (they measure the same).

Whenever your child comes home with a strange, complex geometrical figure, try to break it down into smaller shapes with well-defined properties. For example, a trapezoid looks strange, but you can always break it down into a rectangle with two right triangles on each end. This is a good first step for many geometry problems.

2)   Adjacent inside angles of a parallelogram are supplementary (they add up to 180°).

Applying these rules with the parallelogram above, we see that angle A = angle C, and angle B = angle D. Angles A and B add up to 180°, and angles C and D add up to 180°. Also, angles B and C add up to 180°, as do angles A and D.

A Word on Solids

Your child will be asked to spend some time computing the **surface area** and **volume** of various solid shapes. There are many different solid shapes, and the various formulas attached to them can get pretty complicated. See your child's textbook or a homework website (see page 163) for the necessary formulas when a question on solids comes up.

Data Analysis and Probability

Data Analysis

Data Analysis usually refers to graphs and visual information, but it also covers number-crunching concepts like mean, median, mode, and range.

Mean

Mean is what most people are referring to when they talk about finding the average of a group of numbers.

EXAMPLE:

If your child had the following quiz scores:

4, 7, 7, 7, 9, 9, 10, 10, 12, 17, 18

what is his mean score?

To find the mean, you would need to add up all the scores, and then divide this number by the number of quizzes.

Mean = (4 + 7+ 7 + 7 + 9 + 9+ 10 + 10 + 12 + 17 + 18)

$$\div\ 11\ [\text{quizzes}] =$$

$$110 \div 11 = 10$$

The mean (average) of the test scores is 10.

Mode

The mode refers to the number that appears most often in a set of numbers.

EXAMPLE:

What is the mode of the quiz scores listed previously?

Since there are three 7s in the quiz scores, the mode of the test scores is 7.

Median

The median can be found by listing all the numbers from least to greatest (this has already been done), and then finding the number that is in the middle.

If there were only ten quiz scores, to find the median you would take the middle two numbers—the fifth and sixth numbers—and then split the difference between them. If you lop off the 18 in the quiz scores, then the middle two numbers are 7 and 9, so the median would be 8.

EXAMPLE:

What is the median score of the scores listed previously?

There are eleven test scores above—we knew that from finding the mean—so if you count over to the sixth number, you will have the number that has five numbers greater than it, and five numbers fewer than it. The median of this group is nine.

Range

The range of a group is merely the smallest and the largest numbers, so the range for this group is 4 to 18.

Graphs and Charts

Mathematical information displayed in a graph form provides an added quality that abstract numbers cannot. Understanding that 7 is greater than 5 is fairly easy for all of us, but even a very young child can look at the pie graph below and tell you which side is larger.

That is the allure of graphs, and your child will definitely get her fill of charts (also referred to as tables) and graphs in junior high math.

EXAMPLE:

Let's say your child went out each morning and counted the number of caterpillars and beetles he found on the elm tree. How would you place the information he gathered in chart form?

Your child's chart might look like this:

Days of the Week	Caterpillars	Beetles
Monday	2	6
Tuesday	3	6
Wednesday	4	2
Thursday	7	4
Friday	8	5

There is the data in an easy-to-read form, but it still lacks a visual element. In order to provide this, let's take this information and place it into a pie graph, a line graph, and a bar graph.

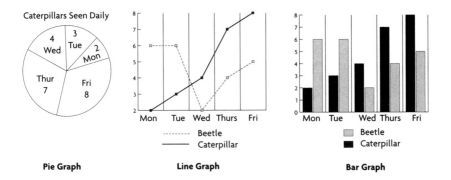

Pie Graph   **Line Graph**   **Bar Graph**

If your child has trouble reading graphs, make sure that she is paying close attention to the key and the labeling of the horizontal and vertical axes. In the line graph, believing that the dotted line stands for the caterpillar sightings will lead to incorrect answers. Also, getting an accurate number on a graph requires some diligence. For instance, if your child is looking to find the number of beetle sightings on Wednesday, she should go along the horizontal axis until directly over Wednesday, and then head straight up. Once she gets to the right line, she should head straight across to the left to find the number. This is fairly obvious, but sloppy graph reading will lead to inaccurate answers.

Each graph uses the same information from the chart and displays it in a different way. The **pie graph** shows how many caterpillars were seen each day—it is helpful in showing which days were the best days. Just by taking a quick glance, your child should be able to discern that Thursday and Friday accounted for the majority of sightings.

The pie is useful to show how each day relates to the entire number of caterpillars seen. If you want to look at how the bug sighting went over time, a **line graph** is very helpful. Looking at the middle graph, you and your child can easily see that caterpillar sightings increased steadily, while beetle sightings dropped during the middle of the week. Line graphs are a good way of showing a pattern developing over time, and while you can compare caterpillar sightings with beetle sightings on it, the **bar graph** does this the best. On this graph, the ability to compare caterpillar to beetle sightings is very distinct. Beetles were ahead early in the week, but caterpillars surged ahead later. The difference in amount can be seen each day by comparing the difference in the shaded and outlined bars for each day.

Probability

Probability problems will probably appear in two main forms. The first kind of probability question asks your child to figure out how many different combinations of something might occur, such as

---

EXAMPLE:

A child rolls a six-sided die three times. How many different combinations are possible?

To answer this, take the number of different outcomes for each die roll, and then multiply them together. On the first roll, there are six possible outcomes: a 1, 2, 3, 4, 5, or 6 will be rolled. This is true for each roll, so the total number of possible combinations becomes 6 (possible outcomes on first roll) × 6 (possible outcomes on second roll) × 6 (possible outcomes on third roll) = 6 × 6 × 6 = 216.

If you add two coin flips to the above question, then you will have 216 × 2 (possible outcomes on the first toss, since it will be either heads or tails) × 2 (possible outcomes on the second toss) = 216 × 2 × 2 = 864 possible combinations.

This is a simpler form of probability question. The harder type deals with **odds:**

EXAMPLE:

A six-sided die is rolled three times. What are the odds that the five will be rolled three consecutive times?

To help answer an "odds" question, let us bring back an idea we discussed at the beginning of the chapter: the fraction. An odds questions breaks down to

Numerator = the number of times the event might occur
Denominator = the total number of outcomes

There are six sides to the die, and only one of them is a 5, so there is only a 1 in 6, or ⅙ chance of it occurring the first time you roll the die. The second roll has the same odds, ⅙, as does the third. So the odds of rolling a 5 three consecutive times are

⅙ × ⅙ × ⅙ = ¹⁄₂₁₆, or 1 in 216.

Here's one more toughie:

EXAMPLE:

A six-sided die is rolled three times. What are the odds that are first roll will be an even number, the second roll will be 3, and the third roll will be greater than 4?

In this question, the numerator will change for each roll, although the denominator stays the same because there are still only six possible outcomes each roll. In the first roll, there are three even numbers (2, 4, and 6), so the odds are ³⁄₆. The second roll is only a one in six chance, but there are two numbers greater than four (5 and 6), so the third roll will have a ²⁄₆ chance of being greater than 4. The odds are then

³⁄₆ × ⅙ × ²⁄₆ = ½ × ⅙ × ⅓ = ¹⁄₃₆, or 1 in 36.

CHAPTER 3

A Review of Key

Junior High English Concepts

 ENGLISH—ALSO CALLED ENGLISH LANGUAGE ARTS in some areas of the country—can be broken down into four main subject areas: Grammar, Reading, Literary Analysis, and Writing. In this chapter we will cover these four main subjects areas, and then talk about the long-term homework project that combines them all in a neat package: the research paper.

Grammar Skills

If a large pharmaceutical company developed a pill that, once swallowed, would give everyone perfect grammar skills, there would be a long line of people waiting at the door with tall glasses of water in their hands (and the authors of this book would be among them).

Homework Heroics: Teaching Kids to Love Reading

THE SINGLE MOST important thing you can do to improve your child's English skills is to encourage your child to read as much as possible. While it would be fabulous if your child decided to read Plato's Republic on her own, it probably is not going to happen, and you shouldn't sweat it. Reading pretty much any kind of book or magazine—whether it's a romance novel or wrestling magazine—is better than not reading at all. The more exposure children get to books, the more comfortable they become both with reading and writing.

Reading provides children with good language models. They see with their eyes and hear in their inner ear (the inner ear you "hear" words with when you read) correctly written sentences put together in moving and interesting ways. This helps your child actually internalize the rules of grammar. She will develop the ability to look at a sentence and determine almost instinctively if it's written correctly, because she knows what correct prose looks like.

A great deal of English grammar contradicts itself; on some levels it's fairly coherent, but on other levels it's seemingly illogical. Here is some advice for both you and your child:

•••••

Understand the basics of grammar—subject/verb agreement, proper capitalization and spelling, for example—and look up anything you do not know in a grammar reference book.

•••••

Make sure your child has a reputable grammar book on hand— the more exhaustive the better. Once you find a book you and your child like, encourage him to:

1) Use it continuously and aggressively

2) Learn from his mistakes

If you can convince your child to look up grammar rules whenever he is unsure of the correct rule, you will have made an important step in helping your child. The next step is to get your child to understand his own errors. Here is one way to make sure this happens:

•••••

Maintain a list called "Common Grammar Mistakes," and have your child jot down one or two, along with the correct grammar rule, whenever he receives a rough draft back from you or a final draft back from the teacher with mistakes highlighted.

•••••

Homework Heroics: Be a Good Model

IT MAY BE a pain to mind your grammar when you are just relaxing at home, but if you provide your child with a good spoken language model at all times, you will be doing him a great service. First of all, by speaking grammatically, you help your child internalize the rules of grammar. Secondly, by speaking correctly yourself, you encourage your child to speak correctly, too, which will set him on the road to success in life. Remember your own mother correcting you whenever you said "ain't"? Well, she had the right idea.

English grammar rules evolved over time. The same should happen with your child, with his knowledge of correct grammar being built on a steady succession of mistakes corrected.

The Eight Parts Of Speech

All words in the English language can be placed into one of eight categories, so a solid understanding of them is critical. So without further ado . . .

Nouns—A noun names a person, place, thing, or idea in a sentence. *Nutmeg, Mrs. Parkinson, happiness*, and *philosophy* are all examples of nouns.

There are two main categories of nouns: common nouns and proper nouns. A **common noun** is any member of a group of persons, places, or things. *Neighbor, house,* and *beach* are all common nouns. A **proper noun** names a specific member of a common group, so *Mrs. Parkinson*, the *White House*, and *Brighton Beach* are all proper nouns. Proper nouns are always capitalized.

Pronouns—A pronoun is a word that takes the place of a noun or another pronoun in a sentence. *I, he, we, everyone,* and *several* are examples of pronouns.

A **personal pronoun** takes the place of persons or things. *I, you, he, she, it, we, us, they,* and *them* are examples of personal pronouns. **Indefinite pronouns** don't substitute for specific nouns; instead, they function as nouns themselves. *All, any, each, everybody, one, someone,* and *several* are all indefinite pronouns. Some indefinite pronouns, like *everyone, someone, none,* and *each* are singular; others, like *few* and *several,* are plural. Some, maddeningly, can be either depending on the context—*all, most,* and *some* are examples. These pronouns cause students no end of grief when it comes to pronoun agreement.

EXAMPLE:

In the following two sentences, underline the correct pronoun:
Everyone should pack (his/their) own lunch.
Few people I know make (her/their) beds every day.

When your child sees one of these tricky indefinite pronouns, tell her to be on guard! She must determine if the pronoun is singular or plural before answering a question like this. The only foolproof ways to do this are either by looking up the answer in a grammar book every time (a cumbersome, but effective, process) or simply memorizing the indefinite pronouns. We recommend the second approach. In the sentences above, *everyone* is a singular indefinite pronoun, so all the other pronouns in the sentence referring to *everyone* should also be singular; that means, "Everyone should pack his own lunch." In the second sentence, we see *few,* which is a plural indefinite pronoun; that means, "Few people I know make their beds every day."

Pronouns come in many shapes and sizes. However, the key point is that they are used in place of a noun or pronoun, and the noun or pronoun they replace is known as the **antecedent**.

Verbs—Verbs are words that express action, occurrence, or state of being. There are two main types of verbs: action verbs and linking verbs. **Action verbs**, as you might expect, express an action that someone or something is taking. "Lester jumped from his chair" contains the action verb *jumped*. A **linking verb** does not express action; instead, it links the subject of a sentence with its **complement**, which is a word or phrase that renames or defines the subject in some way. "Joanie is a juggler" contains the verb *is*, but it does nothing except link the subject, *Joanie,* to its complement, *juggler.* Common linking verbs often include a form of the verb *to be*, or are related to the senses *(look, feel)* or a state of being *(seem, become)*.

Verb Tenses

The tense of a verb refers to time and duration of the action:

The **simple tense** of a verb indicates that an event is present, past, or future in relation to the speaker:

- Present tense: *I write this book.*

- Past tense: *I ate roast beef yesterday for lunch.*

- Future tense: *I will call my mother tomorrow.*

The **perfect tense** of a verb indicates an action or condition that has been completed; it uses a form of the verb *to have:*

- Present perfect: *I have finished my chores.*

- Past perfect: *I had called her that morning.*

- Future perfect: *I will have scraped my bubblegum off the telephone by the time father comes home.*

The **progressive tense** of a verb shows a state or action that is ongoing or in progress; it uses some form of the verb *to be.*

- Present progressive: *I am sleeping.*

• Past progressive: *I was mowing the lawn.*

• Future progressive: *I will be playing basketball all day long.*

*T*he words a, an, and the *are a group of adjectives known as* **articles**. *The word* the *refers to a specific person, place, or thing, so it is usually called a* **definite article**. *The words* a or an *refer to general nouns, so they are called* **indefinite articles**.

Adjectives—Adjectives are words that describe or **modify** a noun or pronoun. The word *modify* means "limits," or "restricts". For example, in the sentence, "That red, four-door car in the parking lot is mine," the adjectives *red* and *four-door* modify the word *car*, limiting the number of cars in the parking lot that the speaker could be referring to. Adjectives usually answer these questions: Which one? What kind? How many? The adjectives in the example above help answer the question, "Which car is mine?"

Adverbs—Adverbs are words that modify a verb, adjective, or another adverb. Adverbs answer questions like: How? How much? Where? When? Many adverbs are created by taking an adjective, like *slow*, and adding *-ly* to it to make the adverb *slowly*. In the sentence, "The rollercoaster moved quickly," the word *quickly* modifies the verb *moved*. In the sentence, "He calls often," *often* describes how frequently he calls.

Prepositions—Prepositions are words that usually show the relationship between a noun or pronoun and other words in the sentence. *By, into, on, between,* and *for* are all prepositions. The noun that is combined with a preposition is referred to as the **object of the preposition**. A **prepositional phrase** is made up of a preposition, the object of the preposition, and an adjective or two that modify the subject of the sentence. So in the sentence, "The baseball on the shelf is dirty," *on* is the preposition, *shelf* is the object, and the whole group of words *on the shelf* is the prepositional phrase.

Conjunctions—Conjunctions are words used to combine or connect words or groups of words together. *And* and *but* are two of the most common conjunctions. *Or, nor, for,* and *yet* are also conjunctions.

Interjections—Interjections are words that express excitement and emotion. They are usually punctuated by an exclamation point, or by a comma when the feeling's not as strong. In the sentence, "Ouch! That stings," the interjection *ouch* shows it really did sting. Words like *alas, yikes, hey*, and *wow* are also interjections.

Sentence Structure and Diagramming

Although most students think the act of diagramming sentences was created as torture, the fact is that diagramming is a very useful way to make sure students understand how a sentence—and the relationships between the different parts of a sentence—works by providing a visual representation of its structure. This is why diagramming is still taught; the better your child understands diagramming, the better he will be at grammar.

Let us talk about the simplest sentence possible to show you the idea behind diagramming. Every sentence has to have at least two parts: a subject and a predicate. The part of the sentence that contains the main noun or pronoun is called the **subject**, while the part that contains the verb is called the **predicate**.

The simple sentence, "The girl walks," contains one noun and one verb, and it is diagrammed like this:

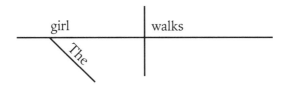

The vertical line through the horizontal line separates the subject from the predicate.

Modifiers go on slanted lines under the words they modify, so the word *the* in the sentence above modifies *girl*. If we also wanted to modify the noun *girl* with the adjective *tall*, it would look like this:

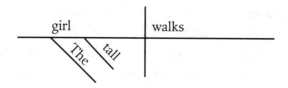

If we decided to add *the boy* to the subject, we would use a conjunction, and both *boy* and *girl* would have to be combined properly with the verb *walks* since they are both walking.

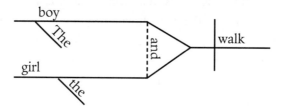

By adding the boy, we now have two subjects, and this changes the singular verb *walks* to the plural word *walk*. Improper subject/verb agreement is a common mistake, so when looking over your child's homework always be on the lookout for it.

Reading and Reading Comprehension

Although there are infinite gradations of understanding, for simplicity's sake we can break reading comprehension into two major levels: basic and advanced. A basic understanding is what your child's teachers focused on in elementary school, and it means that your child understands the nouns and verbs in any particular sentence. If someone were to say, "Beth owns one thousand spoons," your child would understand that Beth is a person, and she would also know the meaning of the words *owns* and *spoons*. An advanced reading comprehension level is the ability to interpret shades of meaning and draw conclusions from information in a text.

Basic Reading Comprehension: Building a Better Vocabulary

Understanding the literal meaning of the words in a sentence is the basic level of reading comprehension, and without it your child will struggle through most English assignments. The main block to this basic level of reading comprehension is an insufficient vocabulary, so by all means. . .

• • • • •

Make sure your child has access to a dictionary when doing English homework.

• • • • •

Sometimes kids are reluctant to stop and look up words they don't know because doing so takes extra time, and they would prefer to finish their homework as quickly as possible. It is important that you help your child overcome this reluctance.

Your child's teacher will probably use several methods to help your child learn new words and understand the relationship between words. In addition to asking her to memorize the definitions, your child's teacher will spend some time working with synonyms, antonyms, homonyms, homophones, homographs, prefixes, suffixes, and word roots. Building strength in these areas helps your child become a better reader and writer. Below are definitions and examples of these terms, so you can help your child with any assistance she might need:

Synonyms—Words that have the same or almost the same meaning. *Big* and *large, wash* and *cleanse, pretty* and *attractive* are all pairs of synonyms.

Antonyms—Two words that have opposite or nearly opposite meanings. *Hot* and *cold, near* and *far, expensive* and *cheap* are all pairs of antonyms.

Homographs—Words that are spelled the same way, but have a different pronunciation and meaning. For example, a *bow* is a decoration you put on a gift, and *bow* is what you do in front of an audience at the end of a play.

Homonyms—Words that sound alike and are spelled the same way but have different meanings. *Park,* as in a nice place to have a picnic, and *park,* as in what you do with your car at the supermarket, are a pair of homonyms.

Homophones—Words that sound alike, but are spelled differently and have different meanings. *Blew* and *blue, principal* and *principle, main* and *mane* are all pairs of homophones.

Prefixes—A syllable or group of syllables added to the beginning of a word to modify the word or change its meaning. Common prefixes include *un-, in-, anti-, mis-, non-, bi-,* and *de-.*

Suffixes—A syllable or group of syllables added to the end of a word to modify the word or change its meaning. Common suffixes include *-able, -ible, -ed, -ify,* and *-ment.*

Word Origins—Many prefixes and suffixes have foreign origins. For example, *tele-* is from a Greek word meaning *far,* so our word *television* really means *far vision*—which is, in fact, what television provides for us. *Micro-* is from a Latin word meaning small, so the word *microscope* can be defined as *small-seer.*

Many dictionaries have long tables of word parts and their meanings. Review these with your child.

Homework Heroics: The Shared Parts Games

IF YOU HEAR yourself or your child use a word that has a common word part in it, work together to come up with as many other words that share that word part as you can. For example, if your child says that a particular classmate is "insensitive," try to come up with other words that use the prefix *in-.* If your child demands that you stop "micromanaging" her, ask her to come up with some other *micro-* words.

Understanding Words from Context

An important aspect of basic reading comprehension at the junior-high level is learning to decipher the meaning of a word from the clues in the sentence in which it appears, or in the sentences around that sentence. If your child doesn't understand a word in a story or assignment she is reading, try asking her questions to help her focus on the clues surrounding the unknown word. For example: "After eating nothing for the past three days besides some mints he had found in his pockets, the ravenous boy could hardly believe his luck when he stumbled upon a campfire and saw three huge trout roasting on a stick." If your child doesn't know what the word *ravenous* means, you might ask her, "Why was the boy excited to find the fish?" "How would you feel if the only thing you'd had to eat in three days were some old mints?" By asking these types of questions, you can help your child discover that *ravenous* means "extremely hungry."

Advanced Reading Comprehension: Interpreting Reading Material

Basic reading comprehension skills are essential in order to progress to the advanced level of reading comprehension. Advanced reading comprehension means that your child is able to read a sentence or paragraph and then draw conclusions and make interpretations that go beyond the literal meaning of the words.

Junior high students will be expected not only to understand the words on the page but to think and write critically about books, stories, and articles.

Reading complex technical documents and reading fiction require slightly different kinds of strategies, but both fall under the heading of Literary Analysis.

Literary Analysis

Many terms are used when talking about reading selections, and reading selections can vary greatly—from poetry to scientific articles. We will review major literary terms and discuss the major types of literature.

Common Literary Terms

Main Idea or Theme—The main idea or theme is the broad message of the work, an idea that can usually be summed up in a sentence. It is the central belief or principal idea that propels the piece.

EXAMPLE:

What was the main idea of the story?

To help your child come up with a main idea, ask him leading questions such as:

1)   What did you feel like after reading the piece? Were you sad, happy, disturbed?

2)   Was there a central conflict or event in the story? A moral?

3)   Was the story told from a particular point of view? If so, what impact did that point of view have on the meaning of the story?

If your child can explain these things, he will be on the right track. As long as your child can back up his version of the main idea with facts or examples from the story, it should stand up well.

Plot—Basically, if you can summarize the main events or tell what happens in a story, you have its plot.

If your child has trouble recounting the plot of a particular story, it is probably because he read carelessly or quickly. Ask him to read it again, without outside distractions, and encourage him to make notes of major plot points. If your child frequently has trouble recounting a plot, his basic reading comprehension skills may need work. See our discussion of basic reading comprehension starting on page 91. If the problem persists, seek help from your child's teacher.

Characters—These are the people or creatures within a story. For example, in the fable *Little Red Riding Hood,* the characters are Red Riding Hood, the wolf, and Grandma.

*In some stories, characters change emotionally as a story progresses. This progression can be referred to as a **character arc**.*

Setting—The setting is the scenery, location, or period of time in which a story or other work takes place. Going back to the *Little Red Riding Hood* example, the settings of the story are the forest and Grandma's house.

Tone or mood—The tone or mood of a story is the emotional atmosphere set by the author, which is achieved through careful word choice. "It was a dark, windy day," and "the festive party," are examples of how an author uses word choice to establish mood. There can be dark stories about birthday parties and funny stories about prisons—it all depends on the events portrayed and language used.

EXAMPLE:

What are some of the words, phrases, and events in the story that help create its mood?

Your child may get a question like this in order to help him learn about careful language use. For example, certain words have definite **connotations,** which are attitudes or feelings associated with a word in addition to its definition. As your child develops the ability to understand and think critically about the mechanics of a piece of fiction or nonfiction, his advanced reading comprehension and literary analysis skills grow.

If your child is faced with a question like this, ask him to read parts of the story aloud, pausing whenever a certain word or event causes him to feel a particular emotion. Continue asking questions like, "Why did that make you laugh?" or "What about this description is sad/goofy/frightening?" and help your child come up with ways, supported by the text, to back up his answers.

Symbolism—Symbolism refers to the use of a particular object, person, place—or other element of a story or poem—to represent something else. For example, a black cat that appears in a particular story every time the main character is about to commit a crime might symbolize "evil." If the black cat runs away in the end, it might symbolize the main character's overcoming his evil impulses.

Questions about symbolism are often very difficult for junior high school students, mainly because they are only just learning to think beyond the literal level. To help your child discern symbolic representations in a particular story or poem, ask him to list any characters, animals, or objects that feature prominently at key moments in the piece. For example, does the river in a particular book appear always to be the means of escape and salvation for a young boy and his friend? (We're thinking of Huckleberry Finn and Jim here, in case you're curious). In this case, the river might symbolize freedom. Bear in mind an important rule of literary analysis while doing this and other analytical exercises:

·····

There is no one right answer in literary analysis. Your child just needs to be able to support his ideas and interpretations logically, using the text in question for support.

·····

This frustrates some children who like definite answers, but try to encourage your child to see analyzing reading material as a chance to be creative.

Imagery—Imagery is descriptive language that vividly recreates a sensory experience. Imagery might appeal to sight, hearing, smell, or touch. For example, "The icy rain rolled relentlessly down my face, leaving freezing, stinging trails across my exposed flesh," appeals to the sense of touch. "When at last I went inside, I almost wept with joy as the floury, buttery smell of fresh pancakes on the stove comforted me," appeals to the sense of smell.

Simile and Metaphor—Similes and metaphors are figurative uses of language. A simile is figurative language in which two essentially unlike things are compared; they often use the words *like* or *as*. "Fit as a fiddle" and "Mohammed Ali floated like a butterfly," are both similes.

A metaphor is figurative language in which a word or phrase that ordinarily describes one thing is used to describe another, such as "all the world's a stage." Metaphors can also be a little more drawn out and subtle: "The morning fog lapped at the corners of the street, curled its long, gray tail around its haunches, lingered and licked its paws, then scampered back up to the sky to chase the birds." Here, we can see that a cat is used as a metaphor for fog, even though the word *cat* is never specifically used.

EXAMPLE:

Compare story X to story Y (usually based on a particular theme, like "in terms of the treatment of children").

This is a very hard question. To do this, your child will have to understand the characters, plot, main ideas, and literary devices used in two stories, and then explain the similarities and differences. To begin, ask your child to make a note whenever the particular theme appears. Then, ask him to formulate a main idea about the term of comparison in each piece. To prompt him, ask him the same types of questions you would when trying to uncover the overall main idea of a story:

1) After reviewing these scenes, what is your general feeling?

2) Was there a central conflict or event?

3) What is the end result of each story?

4) Do the authors write from similar or different points of view? Do they represent the treatment of children similarly, or do they have different attitudes about the subject?

If your child can explain why he feels the way he does using major literary terms (like character, imagery, etc.), he will have formulated a thesis about the author's treatment of children in the piece. Once he does this for both stories, the hard part is over. Comparison becomes a matter of talking about imagery, characters, and so forth, in the stories that give similar impressions; and imagery, characters, and so forth, that give different impressions.

Major Literary Genres

There are countless categories into which writing can be divided, but at the junior high level, your child need only be concerned with four major categories, or **genres** (pronounced ZHAN - ruhs): non-fiction, fiction, drama, and poetry.

Nonfiction

Nonfiction is factual prose writing (prose is just writing that is not poetry). News articles, essays, history books, biographies, almanacs, reference materials—everything that is not a play or poem and does not involve making up people, places, and events—is nonfiction. Just because nonfiction is factual does not mean that it has to be balanced and fair. In fact, certain types of nonfiction, such as an Op-Ed piece in the newspaper, are very often opinionated and one-sided. Showing your child how to understand an author's motivations and approach nonfiction critically is a major part of the junior high English teacher's job.

If your child is asked to analyze a piece of nonfiction and gets stumped, ask her the following questions:

1. What is this piece about in general?

2. What is the author's attitude towards the subject: reverent, mocking, ironic, amused?

3. What is this piece designed to "do": persuade, inform, arouse a certain emotion, entertain?

4. Who was/is the intended audience for this piece? Scientists? Eighteenth-century British landlords? Teenage girls?

5. Who is the author of this piece, and what do you know about him or her? What are his/her qualifications? What position is he/she taking on the issue (if there is an issue involved)?

6. What kind of tone does the author use? Is it appropriate?

7. What kinds of support does the author use to bolster his or her arguments? Is that support convincing to you? Would it be convincing to the original audience?

8. Based on your answers to the questions above, do you think this piece is effective in doing what it was written to do? Why or why not?

Fiction

Fiction is a class of literature that involves narration in prose form and deals with partly or completely imaginary characters or events. Short stories, novels, and novellas are all works of fiction. As your child progresses through junior high and high school and on into college, analyzing fiction will become the focus of his English classes. The major challenge most junior high students face is that they are not accustomed to questioning the written word. They take what they read at face value. When analyzing fiction, one must be comfortable making supportable judgments and assumptions. Here is one way your child might be asked to approach a work of fiction:

EXAMPLE:

Discuss the impact of [a certain book] in its historical context.

Teachers want to show that the meaning of a text changes depending on the times and people who read it. Books that were considered shocking or revolutionary in their own time are often considered irrelevant or boring by today's young readers (a book like abolitionist Harriet Beecher Stowe's *Uncle Tom's Cabin* is a prime example). Nevertheless, students need to learn to understand works in context.

To help your child address such a question, do a little time-travel exercise. Help him imagine what life was like in 1950s New York, or Elizabethan England, or in this case, pre-Civil War America. He might need to use reference materials to research the period, but you can help by asking questions like:

1) What did people value most at this time? What did they fear the most?

2) What was a typical day like for most people? Does the piece reflect a change in that typical lifestyle or is it a depiction of everyday life?

3) Is some aspect of everyday life being threatened in the story? Extolled?

4) What political/economic/technological factors were at work? Do they have intended or unintended consequences in the story?

5) Were the social and/or moral standards of the day an important factor in the story? How so?

6) Does the author express a point of view that is in favor of or against ideas or practices that were commonly accepted at the time?

Based on his answers to these questions, your child should start to see what kind of impact a certain story or novel might have had on its audience. He may even see how a book that is frequently described today as heavy-handed, such as *Uncle Tom's Cabin,* could have been a bestseller that shocked the country.

There are any number of other approaches to fiction and the approaches will become more complex as your child progress through school. A good starting place, no matter what the required approach, is to look for the main idea and think about the use of major literary devices in the work. See the discussion of literary terms on pages 94-98 for guidelines.

Drama

Dramas are plays. Your child probably will not read much drama in junior high (she will in high school), but she may encounter her first Shakespeare play by eighth grade. Dramas are meant to be performed for audiences, not read, so they tend to be difficult for students to handle. Students don't get the benefit of an actor's interpretation of a role when they read a character's lines, and they have to visualize sets and actions. Make sure your child understands the following general drama terms:

Act—This a major section or segment of a play, much like a chapter in a book. It tends to have its own climax toward the end.

Scene—These are smaller sections within an act. A change from one scene to another usually represents a change in actors on the stage and sometimes a change of set, or a change in how the audience focuses on the set. They may concentrate on two actors on one side of the stage during one scene, then one actor on the other side of the stage during the next scene.

Set—This is the collection of objects, furniture, decorations, and scenery on stage at any given moment. Sometimes playwrights describe the set in detail; at other times, no set description is available.

Stage Direction—These are instructions to the actors about what to do and where to stand on stage. These directions are set off from the actor's lines in various ways. They may be in brackets or italicized.

Homework Heroics: Shakespeare on Tape

IF YOUR CHILD is struggling to read and analyze a play and has some time before the assignment is due, it might help if you can find a reputable production of the play on videotape to show her. Don't rent a "modernized" or "abridged" version. If it's a Shakespeare play she is studying, try to find a PBS or BBC production on tape (many of these are available at major video rental chains). Your child will probably benefit greatly from hearing the actual words of the play spoken. Watch the play with her and talk to her about it afterwards, asking the same kinds of question you would ask when analyzing a work of fiction (see pages 99-100). After she watches the play, make sure she re-reads it. She will now have a good mental image of the events of the play to help her as she reads.

Poetry

Poetry is non-prose writing. There are dozens of terms associated with poetry, but your junior-high student need only be concerned with the basics:

Blank Verse—Verse is another word for poetry. Blank verse is unrhymed, metered poetry. The lines don't rhyme, but there is a definite rhythmic structure.

Free Verse—Free verse is poetry without a fixed metrical or rhyming pattern. Much modern poetry is written in free verse.

Meter—Meter refers to the rhythmic pattern of lines of poetry—which syllables are stressed and which are not. A unit of stressed and unstressed syllables in a line of poetry is called a **foot**. The meter in some poems is very obvious: "I think that I shall never see/A poem lovely as a tree," has a definite da-DUM da-DUM da-DUM da-DUM rhythm.

Rhyme—This is the characteristic most people associate with poetry, and it means that words correspond in sound with one another. For example, *blight* and *plight* rhyme. A great deal of poetry features lines whose final words rhyme in some sort of regular pattern. Your child may be asked to note this pattern.

Sonnet—A sonnet is a very popular, widely studied poetic format. A sonnet is fourteen lines long and is usually written in iambic pentameter. It has a set pattern of rhyme and often deals with a single idea or sentiment. A standard English sonnet is made up of three four-line stanzas following by a couplet, a rhyming pair of lines.

Stanza—A stanza is a group of lines in a poem, usually four or more, arranged in various patterns according to meter or rhyme, and set off from other sections.

The most well-known source of blank verse are Shakespeare's plays, which are written in unrhymed lines of **iambic pentameter**. Iambic pentameter? What is that, you ask? It's one of those many dozens of poetic terms, but since your child might encounter it when studying Shakespeare, here is a quick translation: "pentameter" refers to a line that has five stressed beats, and "iambic" refers to the pattern of stresses. An iamb is an unstressed syllable followed by a stressed syllable: da-DUM.

If your child is asked to analyze a poem, ask him the same kinds of questions you might ask when searching for the main idea and tone of a story (see pages 94-95). He should concentrate on the poet's use of literary techniques such as imagery, metaphor, and simile, and try to determine the purposes they serve.

Writing Skills

On writing assignments, whether they are fiction or nonfiction, you are best off helping your child before he begins, and then letting him write it on his own. Before he starts, though, it's essential that he understands what kind of writing assignment he's being asked to complete. There are several different types of writing assignments your child might encounter, and each requires a slightly different strategy. Major types of writing assignments include:

Creative Writing—Short stories and poems fall into this category. Careful use of language to evoke moods and flesh out characters are important here, but stories need a beginning, middle, and end, so organization is also essential.

Expository Essay—Here, your child will be asked to explain a process or situation, acquaint the reader with a body of knowledge, or describe a problem and its solution. Clarity is key here, so organization will be the main focus.

Informal Essay—Informal essays are often more personal than other essay forms, and they tend to express an opinion or observation. A strong structure and clearly expressed ideas are the most important elements of this kind of essay.

Literary Essay—A literary essay requires your child to explore the meaning and construction of a piece of literature. This will require him to adopt an opinion about how and why a piece was put together in a particular way. Your child will have to pay attention to specific elements like structure, style, and tone, and will be expected to provide examples to support his opinion. See pages 93-98 for more tips on analyzing literature.

Persuasive Essay—In this kind of assignment, your child will be asked to choose one side of an argument, make a case for it, anticipate and address potential counterarguments, and try to prove that his position is the best one. The key to this assignment is to clearly state his position and provide supporting evidence that will outweigh any possible alternative arguments.

You can help with writing assignments by trying to make sure your child follows these steps:

Stage One: The Brainstorming Session and Developing a Topic Sentence

For any assignment more than one page in length, it is helpful to begin by brainstorming about the project. Once your child has a clear idea of the type of assignment she's facing, help her let her imagination loose and think freely to come up with ideas for a topic, or ideas for approaching an assigned topic. Often, bad or off-the-wall ideas can lead to good ones, so keep the ideas flowing and don't criticize.

If your child has a creative writing assignment, the brainstorming session is still important. The crucial concept then is to get your child to clarify the main theme in her story, plot, and characters.

You can use common movie terms to prompt your child along these lines. Ask her, "Who is the Bad Guy in your story, and who's the Good Guy? What do each of these characters do within the story that makes them Good or Bad? Is there a Love Interest? Will there be a Surprise Ending?" (These phrases are being capitalized because that's how movie people think. They think big, baby, in letters 100 feet tall! Okay, let's do lunch.)

Make sure your child writes down the ideas you and she come up with when brainstorming. You don't want to brainstorm ideas one day only to forget what they were on the next.

After the brainstorming session, have your child wait a day if time permits, and then look at her list of ideas. She should select one and refine it into a main idea or topic sentence. Armed with the topic sentence, she should head onward to Stage Two.

Stage Two: Preliminary Research

Note: Your child may skip Stages Two and Three if the assignment is purely creative. If the assignment is expository or persuasive, your child will likely have to muster some facts. It's time for a trip to the library! Encourage your child to:

Cast a Wide Net at First—Using the card catalog and/or an Internet search engine, your child should begin by looking up general information about his topic. For example, if he decided to write a persuasive essay about strengthening air pollution laws, he might want to take a look at some general books on environmentalism first. Then he should do a little preliminary reading with two purposes in mind:

1) To refine and focus his topic to fit the parameters and page length of the assignment. Often, an idea that seems perfect before any research shows itself to be in need of some serious narrowing and tweaking once some facts enter the picture;

2) To learn of other potential sources that may help him. Most nonfiction books have useful bibliographies and footnotes. Your child should skim these resources for titles of books and articles that focus more specifically on his topic.

Refine the Topic—Your child's initial research might make him decide he wants to change his topic. He may even change his opinion. That's fine, of course. The main problem most junior-high students have is coming up with a topic that is narrow enough to be covered in the length assigned. For example, he may set off to the library convinced he wants to write an expository essay about the cause of the conflict between the Israelis and Palestinians. If he is only supposed to write three to five pages, he is going to have some trouble even scratching the surface of this topic. You can help him by asking him to be more specific, to focus on one particular facet of his broad idea; he can do this by asking himself a series of progressively narrower questions or examining the topic from a different perspective.

Hit the Stacks Again—Armed with a narrow, refined topic sentence, your child should gather sources that specifically address his topic. Here is an important tip no student of any age should forget:

•••••
Ask your librarian for help when you need it!
•••••

Your child should not feel he has to flail about helplessly looking for books. If his search is turning up nothing helpful, he should turn to the librarian for assistance.

Stage Three: Note-taking and Fact Gathering

With an armful of books and articles, your child sits down to figure out what she is going to say on her topic. It is essential that she have some sort of method for keeping track of the information she uncovers for two reasons: (1) It is incredibly frustrating when you can't find a particular fact that you need and (2) she will need her notes organized when it comes time to write a bibliography (see guidelines on page 110).

No-nonsense Note-taking

Encourage your child to follow these steps:

1) Get some note cards.

2) Make a card for each different source, writing down all the publication information in standard form (again, see page 110).

3) Draw a symbol or identifying mark on each card.

4) As your child reads, if she sees a fact she wants to use or quote, she should take out a new note card, write the symbol for the source and the page number, then write down the quote, statistic, or any information she wants to use in her paper. She should have a separate, coded note card for each piece of information.

By following this system, your child will keep all her information available and organized. The other benefits of this system will become clear when we discuss rough drafts.

Fact Gathering

Library books and the Internet are not the only sources of information for a paper. Depending on the topic, a survey or interview may be necessary:

Surveys involve designing a set of questions and getting an appropriate audience to answer them accurately. For example, if your child is writing a persuasive essay about changing the menu in the school cafeteria, she may want to survey students who eat in the cafeteria. She can do this by handing out a written form and then collecting it or by asking questions directly and marking the responses herself.

Interviews are helpful when an expert opinion is called for. Eyewitnesses to events and authorities on certain subjects make good interview candidates. If your child plans to do an interview, she must prepare in advance. She should write down a list of specific questions to ask the person. If possible, she should bring along a tape recorder (few junior-high students take notes quickly enough to keep up with a fast talker). Her questions should be as concrete as possible. Instead of "What was it like to be an astronaut?" she should ask, "What training did you have to go through to become an astronaut? What was the most difficult thing you ever had to do as an astronaut? How did you become interested in space exploration?"

Stage Four: Organization and Outlines

Before your child even thinks about starting to write his paper, he should take some time to organize his thoughts. This holds true for both fiction and non-fiction assignments. Two tried-and-true methods for organizing a paper are **outlining** and **mind maps**. Note: for non-fiction assignments your child should consider whether he wants to organize his paper chronologically, in order of importance, or some other organizational format.

Outlines

Even college students and professional writers use outlines to keep themselves focused. Outlines are like instructions that help you get through an essay or story without getting confused. Your child's teacher may require her to learn formal outlining procedures. You have probably seen this before. Here's a review.

Sample Outline

I. A large Roman numeral indicates a large section of a work. For your child, this probably translates into a paragraph. The main topic of the paragraph goes by the numeral.

  A. The main points within the larger sections go next to capital letters.

  B. Write the main points in sentence form.

  C. Here is another main point.

    1. Smaller pieces of information and minor arguments that relate to a particular main point go under that point's letter next to a regular number.

    2. Here's another smaller point.

      a. If you had an even more minor point to make, it would go here, beside a lower-case letter.

      b. Here is another minor point.

        i. If you really wanted to go into fine detail, you can go back to Roman numerals—lower-case this time.

        ii. Here's another very minor point.

II. Second Large Section topic sentence.

  A. Major point.

  B. Major point.

    1. Smaller point

    2. Smaller point

      a. Very small point.

You get the idea. As you move into finer detail, indent and use the next numbering system in the outline.

Even if your child isn't required to develop a formal outline, an informal outline is always a good idea. Simply ask her to think out her paper paragraph by paragraph and write down the main points and facts she intends to include in each paragraph.

Mind Maps

Some folks don't like the restrictions of a linear organizational system like an outline. In recent years, an alternative has gained popularity with teachers and students: mind maps. Don't worry, this doesn't involve hypnosis. Mind maps are visual representations of the relationship of the different pieces of an essay. Here's an example:

Sample Mind Map

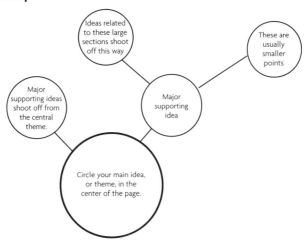

Ideas related to these large sections shoot off this way

These are usually smaller points

Major supporting ideas shoot off from the central theme.

Major supporting idea

Circle your main idea, or theme, in the center of the page.

Stage Five: The Rough Draft

If your child has an outline or mind map and all his note cards together, the rough draft should be a snap. He simply needs to go through his notes and organize the cards to follow along with his outline (some tinkering with the outline may occur at this stage, which is fine). If he has taken thorough notes, writing the rough draft becomes a matter of linking the notes with his own thoughts according to the outline he created.

While writing more than one draft of a paper is an important part of learning to write well, there may be times when your child decides to skip the rough draft—especially if it doesn't have to be turned in. Skipping the rough draft puts extra pressure on the outline to be clear and comprehensive, however, so be sure to stress outlining. When allotting time for homework, do your utmost to emphasize the importance of writing a rough draft.

Two parts of the nonfiction paper that often get neglected until the end are the parenthetical documentation, or footnotes, and the bibliography, or list of works cited. They should be handled during the rough draft stage. Parenthetical documentation and footnotes are alternative ways of showing the reader of a paper where certain information came from. Footnotes appear at the bottom of a page and parenthetical documentation appears within the text, set off in parentheses. If your child uses material from an outside source in his work, he must provide appropriate documentation of the source or he could get in trouble for plagiarizing (using someone else's words or ideas without giving them credit).

A bibliography or list of works cited provides the publication information for all your child's sources, and it is usually included as a list on a separate page at the end of a paper. Your child's teacher will give him specific guidelines for formatting documentation and bibliographies. One of the most commonly used format guidelines for research papers is *The MLA* (Modern Language Association) *Style Manual*. Most English teachers teach MLA format, so it might be worth picking up this short reference book for your child.

Stage Six: Revising

Learning how to revise one's writing is a critical life-long skill. If your child asks you for help at this stage, try giving her a list of questions that follow the guidelines below so she can try revising on her own first. Afterwards you can look it over and gently make additional suggestions.

Nonfiction

At this grade level, the important elements of non-fiction writing that your child might be expected to know include:

- Stating the thesis, purpose, or position of the paper

- Conveying clear and accurate explanations, opinions, or perspectives on the topic

- Using concise and clear language and appropriate tone (many students make the mistake of writing too informally)

- Supporting the thesis with relevant facts, details, examples, or statistics from one or more sources

- Anticipating and addressing potential counterarguments (particularly in persuasive essays)

- Following an appropriate organizational pattern

- Developing a well-supported and clearly stated conclusion

Here are some common mistakes your child should avoid: personal statements that lack convincing support, arguments with unclear underlying logic, and lack of detail.

Fiction

The important elements of fiction writing that your child might be expected to know in junior high include:

- Establishing and developing a compelling plot that has a beginning, conflict, climax, and resolution

- Developing major and minor characters and setting

- Including concrete, interesting language, and well-chosen details to develop plot and character

- Using appropriate fiction devices, such as dialogue, suspense, and symbolism

> **D**etails count! Don't let your child forget to double-check her spelling, grammar, and paragraph structure. Make sure that she has followed all of her teacher's formatting instructions. She would not want a lot of hard work to be overshadowed by careless mistakes.

When you read your child's rough draft of a fiction assignment, you are looking for overall story development. Here are some questions to help guide you: Is the action in the story sufficiently explained? Is the story compelling? Is there sufficient detail?

Developing Clarity

Often when you are reviewing a rough draft, either nonfiction or fiction, the main problem will be that events or supporting ideas are not explained well enough. This is mainly because young writers often think that because they know exactly what they are talking about and what they are trying to say, their readers will, too. This is why you need to coax them to explain themselves further. Say things like, "This sentence is good, but it would help me understand it better if you explained this skateboard maneuver in greater detail." Your child took it for granted that her audience knew about skateboarding, but this is not always the case.

After your child addresses any major problems with her paper, she is done. Ta-da! She can move on to Stage Seven: Turn in Your Paper and Heave a Sigh of Relief.

Long-Term English Projects: The Research Paper

The longest English assignment your child is likely to receive in junior high is a research paper. The guidelines for writing just discussed (see pages 104-111) and in Long-Term Project Planning at the beginning of the book (see pages 40-42) will see your child through such an assignment. There is one added element, however, with which he may need help: time management. Your child must fit all the pieces of the puzzle into an over-arching whole in order to be able to complete the assignment without becoming too stressed out in the process. Leave the actual time elements to him to decide, such as how long he wants to spend on research, but encourage him to err on the side of caution.

Developing and writing out a work schedule will help your child immensely. For example, see if your child can define what reference materials will be used. Are there entire books on the subject? How about magazine articles or websites? Are there any unusual research methods he needs to consider, such as interviews or surveys? For every one of these answers, have your child add a time element. He may soon find that the amount of research he wants to complete will take six months of steady work, and he may be persuaded to narrow his topic.

Finally, if every phase of the research project is completed on time, and if the final result is something to be proud of, be certain your child hears your praise for his accomplishment. Good homework habits should always be rewarded, and while most junior high kids prefer cash (credit cards accepted at some locations), words of encouragement are just as important to their psyches.

CHAPTER 4

A Review of Key Junior High Science Concepts

THERE'S NO GETTING AROUND IT: science deals with facts. A lot of facts. A lot of facts over a wide variety of topics, ranging from gravity to cycles of extinction. So remember, if your child comes to you with a specific scientific question, don't be surprised if you don't know the answer. Just refer to the tips on what to do when stumped by a homework question in chapter one of this book, page 43.

Physical Science

Physical science focuses on the laws that govern the structure of the universe, such as the properties of matter and energy, as well as the interaction between matter and energy.

Matter

Matter is just a scientific way of saying *stuff.* If you really want to be scientific about it, matter is any substance that occupies space and has weight. So a love letter has substance, but love itself does not. Which is to say that love does matter, but it isn't matter.

States of Matter

There are three main states of matter:

1) **Solid**—Matter in solid form holds its own shape and has a definite volume. These molecules don't move around freely— but they do vibrate slightly—because the strong forces between particles hold them in place. If molecules are heated, they will vibrate faster and eventually move farther apart.

2) **Liquid**—A liquid has a definite volume but no fixed shape. The forces between the particles are weaker than a solid, so the molecules move around and assume the shape of the container they are in.

3) **Gas**—A gas is matter that has no definite shape or volume. The molecules are very far apart, so they move about randomly and expand to fill any container they are put into.

You should be aware of the key phrase, *depending on temperature and pressure.* If you mess with these two items, you can change the state of matter.

EXAMPLE:

By what process can you convert water into a gas? By what process can you convert it into a solid?

The answer to this question is based on common experience. To convert water to gas, heat it to the boiling point. At that point, it starts to become steam or vapor, the gaseous form of water. The temperature is the key factor here. Heat speeds up the molecules' movement and gets them bouncing around randomly like a gas. To convert water to a solid, temperature is again key. If you took water and placed it into your freezer, you would exert a different kind of temperature on it. This changes liquid water into ice, a solid. The principle is pretty much the same with other sorts of matter. Rock can become hot liquid magma spewing out of a volcano if it is heated to the right temperature (thankfully, your child can't try this experiment on your stovetop). If chilled to the right temperature, the gas nitrogen can become liquid and be used by your doctor to freeze warts off your skin. Air pressure affects the rates of all these processes; the more pressure that's applied, the cooler molecules become.

Now that we understand matter and its different states, let's talk about the types of matter in the world and the scientific terms used to describe matter:

Atoms—All matter is made up of smaller units called atoms, which are really, really, really small. An atom is the smallest particle of an element that still retains that element's chemical properties. Atoms are composed of a nucleus, protons, neutrons, and electrons.

The **nucleus** is the central core of an atom, and it contains protons and neutrons, as well as most of the atom's mass. The nucleus has a positive charge.

A **proton** is a positively charged particle that makes up part of the nucleus of an atom. A **neutron** is an uncharged particle in the nucleus of an atom. **Electrons** are negatively charged atomic particles that are much lighter than either neutrons or protons. They orbit around the nucleus.

If an atom gains or loses an electron, its charge is unbalanced and it becomes a charged atom called an **ion**.

The attraction between the positively charged protons and negatively charged electrons holds the atom together and makes it electrically neutral.

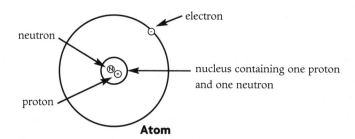

Atom

Think of the nucleus as a clubhouse, and the proton and neutron are the club members. The neutron has no charge (such self-confidence is alluring), while the proton has a positive charge. The electron has a negative charge, and it's a runt compared to the other particles; because of this it does not get to come into the nucleus clubhouse, and must instead orbit around outside, constantly saying stuff like, "C'mon, guys, let me in!"

There are things known as subatomic particles (with such wacky names as quarks and leptons) that are even smaller than protons, neutrons, and electrons, but your child will not have to go anywhere near these topics until college. Be thankful for this.

Elements—An element is a class of matter that cannot be broken down into simpler parts by chemical means; it is a substance that contains only one kind of atom. Some common elements are hydrogen, oxygen, carbon, lead, and mercury. The number of electrons and protons in an atom of any particular element will always be equal, but the number of neutrons may vary slightly.

Many times, people get the terms atom *and* molecule *mixed up. Just remember that atoms are the smallest unit, so while one molecule can be formed of different atoms, an atom can't be made of different molecules.*

Molecules—A tiny structure composed of two or more atoms held together by a bond. Compounds and some elements contain molecules.

You see, the reason you use the phrase *molecule of water* is because a molecule of water is a different type of matter than either hydrogen or oxygen. Have you ever noticed that marriage sometimes changes two people? You knew the people when they were single, but now that they've married they're completely different? Well, the same theory works at the atomic level. By combining two atoms of hydrogen with one atom of oxygen, you get a new molecule—water—that has a whole new set of chemical properties. The same is true of all molecules. They have characteristic properties that differ from the properties of their constituent elements.

Compounds—A compound is a substance formed by the chemical combination of atoms of two or more elements. A compound has properties that are different from its constituent elements. Salt is a compound made of sodium and chlorine.

Types of Compounds

Compounds come in many categories, but in grades six through eight your child will focus mainly on acids, bases, and neutrals.

Scientifically speaking, an **acid** is a compound that forms hydrogen ions when dissolved in water. This definition doesn't really help you form a clear picture in your head, though, does it? More concretely, very strong acids, like the hydrochloric acid in your stomach, are corrosive, and weak acids, like citric acid in lemon juice, have a sour or sharp taste. Vinegar is another example of a weak acid.

A **base** is a compound that neutralizes an acid and forms OH⁻ ions when dissolved in water. Strong bases, like strong acids, are corrosive. Common bases include ammonia and lye. Bases that can be dissolved in

A chemical reaction, such as burning, creates a change in the composition of a substance, causing it to become a new substance with different properties. These changes usually involve the release or absorption of energy. The binding of two atoms of hydrogen with one atom of oxygen is a familiar chemical change that makes water, our beloved H_2O.

water are called *alkalis,* and the level of "base-ness" of a base is often referred to as its *alkalinity.*

A **neutral** is neither acidic nor basic.

Compounds are usually best visualized on something called the pH scale with acids at one end, neutrals in the middle, and bases on the other end. The **pH scale** measures the acidity or alkalinity (non-acidity) of a compound on a scale from zero to 14. A neutral has a pH of 7; an acid is less than 7; and a base has a pH greater than 7.

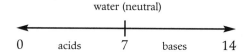

Many chemical reactions between elements create compounds, but this isn't always the case. Sometimes you mix two elements together, and while the molecules swirl around each other, no chemical reaction takes place, and the substances can be easily separated again. This is called a **mixture**, and the best analogy is the chocolate chip cookie. If you pretend cookie dough is one element and chocolate chips are another, you end up with a delicious Mixture Cookie. Think about it: you can pluck out each chip as you get to it, and it hasn't changed in taste or texture since when it was alone. The same goes for the cookie dough.

Motion

Motion occurs everywhere, from asteroids hurtling through space to tiny molecules bouncing around. Probably the guy who studied motion more than anyone else in his time was Sir Isaac Newton. He studied motion so much he was able to form three famous laws about it.

Newton's Laws of Motion
1. Unless acted on by an external force, an object at rest stays at rest, and a moving body continues moving at the same speed in the same straight line.

A **force** is an influence that changes the state of rest or motion of a body. Therefore, if you leave a baseball at rest on a table, it will never move. This principle is called **inertia**, which is the resistance of an object to a change in motion, and it explains why your child sometimes spends five hours on the couch watching television even though there's nothing on. He started watching television, and until something comes along and changes his pattern (such as you telling him to do his homework), he won't stop.

2. An external force applied to a body gives it an acceleration proportional to the force (and in the direction of the force) and inversely proportional to the mass of the body.

Mass is the amount of matter in a body. In simpler terms, the first part of this law says, "the harder you throw the baseball, the faster it will go." The second part states that heavier objects (objects with greater mass) are harder to throw than lighter objects. So if you used the same amount of force to throw a baseball and a bowling ball, the bowling ball won't travel as far, because it has greater mass.

3. For every action there is an equal and opposite reaction.

For example, when the cue ball strikes another ball on a pool table, the struck ball can exert a force on the cue ball that sends it rolling backward.

Gravity and Friction

Newton's laws provide a good general understanding of how objects interact in motion. Two other concepts, gravity and friction, also help this understanding. All objects with mass exert a force on other objects. **Gravity** is the force of attraction between two bodies. Gravity is strong only when something has a large mass, and it gets stronger as the distance between two bodies decreases. So, if the object is a breath mint, you don't stand a big chance of being drawn into its gravitational field, unable ever to break free. However, if the object is something like the earth, you will feel its gravitational pull. This pull is what keeps your feet on the ground, or why you land after jumping up. Because the gravitational pull of the earth is constant, you can drop two objects with different masses (say a feather and your trusty bowling ball), and they will fall to the earth at the same rate of speed, neglecting other factors.

The "neglecting other factors" has to be added because if you try the above experiment, you will find the bowling ball hits the ground first (be sure to move your feet before this happens). The feather floats down. This is because air friction affects the two objects differently. **Friction** is defined as a force that opposes the motion of two bodies in contact; it acts against the direction of motion, causing objects to slow down or stop. In the case of the feather, the two bodies are the feather and the air itself. Contact with the air slows the feather down on its descent.

*T*o see friction in action, get a large piece of sandpaper, a regular piece of paper, and a marble. Roll the marble gently on both pieces of paper. The bumps on the sandpaper will slow down the marble. This is friction in action.

Energy

Energy is the capacity to do work or be active. Energy comes in many different forms. For example, a baseball resting on a high shelf has **potential energy,** which is energy derived from position rather than motion; it is energy that is stored until the object is released. In this case, if the baseball rolled off the shelf, it would convert its potential energy into **kinetic energy**—the energy of a moving object—as it plummeted towards the floor. If you picked up the baseball and placed it back on the shelf, you would be using up kinetic energy but the baseball would be gaining potential energy. When this happens, you should note that one form of energy is being replaced with another. This has to do with an important concept, the **Conservation of energy principle,** which states:

Energy cannot be created or destroyed. Energy can be converted from one form to another, but the total quantity of energy in a system remains the same.

That's why you have to keep putting gas in your car (which the car engine converts into the energy that turns the wheels), food in your mouth (which your stomach breaks down into chemical compounds that your body's cells convert into fuel), and wood on a fire (if you want to remain warm, that is).

*T*he conserva-tion of energy principle is also referred to as the **conservation of mass and energy**, because if mass is converted into energy, the same quantity of mass and energy in the system remains the same.

Do you know the formula for this conversion? I bet you and your child have heard of it: Energy = Mass × (the speed of light) × (the speed of light). Since the speed of light is often designated by the variable c, this equation becomes

$$E = mc^2.$$

Life Sciences

*W*hile physical science concerns itself with the Small Picture (atoms and such), much of life sciences is about the Big Picture. Items like food chains, Earth's ecosystems, and the cycle of water on Earth are key topics in this branch of science.

The Food Chain

To begin with, a brief discussion of an ecosystem is in order. An **ecosystem** is formed by the interaction of a community of organisms with its environment (including non-living things). A **food chain** is the path that nutrients take in an ecosystem, where each member of the sequence of organisms feeds on the member below it. There are different food chains depending on climate, which is just an obvious way of saying animals in a desert do not eat or live the same way as animals in a rainforest. Here are two basic facts that relate to most food chains:

1) Most food chains begin with plants using sunlight, water, and minerals from the soil to grow.

2) All food chains end in the same place that they started.

Think of the life cycle of a tasty little flower. It started off as a plant in a field, which grew using **chlorophyll**—the substance that makes plant leaves green—to convert sunlight, water, and minerals in the soil into energy. This plant was then eaten by a rabbit, which broke down the cellulose of the plant to use as energy for its own growth. A fox then came along, and since foxes eat meat, the rabbit provided the fox with a meal. Eventually, this fox dies, and its body ends up in a field. In time the body decomposes, adding a layer of minerals to the soil. These minerals are combined by a tasty little flower with water and sunlight to create the energy it uses to grow, and everything starts over again.

Most food chains follow the pattern: plant → herbivore (plant-eater) → small carnivore (meat-eater) → larger carnivore → large carnivore dies, providing minerals for plants.

Throughout the whole process, energy is never destroyed, it just changes forms (similar to the conservation of mass and energy principle on pages 122-123). Sunlight was used by the plant, plant matter was used by the rabbit, and the rabbit was eaten by the fox. Overall, if you were to measure the quantity of energy in the system, you would find it unchanged.

Organisms

Besides the environmental Big Picture, life sciences also focus on the **organisms**—that is, all living things, including plants and animals—that make up all environments.

Microscopic Organisms—There are organisms so small that they can't even be seen by the naked eye. These living beings can be as small as a single-celled organism. **Protozoa** make up a large group of single-celled microscopic organisms, including everybody's favorite single-celled organism, the amoeba. An **amoeba** is a one-celled clump of goo that has no definite form, eats by engulfing its food, and moves by using pseudopods. Little creatures like the amoeba are all around us, especially in our water systems. **Bacteria** are also single-celled, or uni-cellular, organisms.

Large Organisms—Your child will spend more time learning about big animals—say ant-sized and up—than microscopic animals in grades 6-8. The first thing she will be confronted with is the **system of classification of organisms** (sometimes called *taxonomy*) that organizes all plants and animals into the following categories:

Kingdom, Phylum, Class, Order, Family, Genus, and Species

In biology, organisms are classified in increasingly specific categories, so a kingdom is the broadest category and a species is the most specific.

For example, humans belong to the kingdom *Animalia,* which means we are animals, not plants (*Plantae* is another major kingdom). Our phylum is *Chordata,* indicating that we have backbones, unlike other animals such as slugs and jellyfish. Our class is *Mammalia,* which (and you probably guessed this already) means we are mammals, a distinction we share with other animals that nurse their babies and have warm blood (among other mammalian characteristics). *Primates* is our order, while *Hominidae* is our family. *Homo* is our genus, and *Sapiens* is our species. Scientists generally refer to organisms by their genus and species, so humans are *Homo sapiens.* The system of classification of organisms is often hard to remember in order, so here is a handy way for your child to memorize them. This sentence gives the first letter of the part of the classification system:

•••••

King Philip Called Out For Ginger Snaps.

••••••

Your child will learn broad characteristics of certain groups of plants and animals and be asked to draw conclusions about other plants and animals based on what he learns. Here is an example of the kind of question he might encounter on his homework or as part of a class discussion:

EXAMPLE:
What kind of food do you think this animal would eat? Explain your reasons.

If you are confronted with a question like this from your child, your best bet would be to review his notes and textbook before starting to work. This gives you an idea of the subject matter your child has been dealing with and will tip you off to the kind of answer his teacher seeks. In this case, the question seems to be asking the student to determine whether the animal with this head was a meat-eater (carnivore), a plant-eater (herbivore), or an equal-opportunity eater of plants and animals (omnivore). This particular animal has huge, sharp teeth and large jaws. Such a mouth is not necessary for attacking grass and leaves. It would be a good guess to say the animal was a carnivore, since sharp teeth are needed for tearing meat.

On the other hand, if the animal's skull had large eye sockets set on opposite sides of its head, your child could conclude that the animal was an herbivore; it spent a lot of time grazing on grass and plants, but it also needed to watch out for predators, so its eyes were as big as possible and covered the greatest range of vision.

Life Cycles and Reproduction

Your child will be taught a bit about the birds and the bees in junior high or, more likely, the earthworms and the butterflies, two favorite exemplars of these topics. That's right, she will figure out how certain baby animals are made and what stages they go through as they develop.

Life Cycles

Here is where the butterflies come in, although your child may focus on any number of other animals, including humans. Unfamiliar terms likely to arise are:

Larva—An early stage in the development of an insect that undergoes metamorphosis, in which the insect is wingless and primarily occupied with feeding.

Pupa—The non-feeding stage between the larva and adult, during which an insect transforms into an imago within a protective cocoon or chrysalis (see below).

Chrysalis—The hard, protective shell in which moth and butterfly pupas spend their development period.

Metamorphosis—Process by which certain animals undergo a change in form, structure, or function, by a natural process of development.

Imago/Adult—An adult insect, ready to take on all his insect duties.

Reproduction

Reproduction is the process by which plants or animals produce offspring. There are two types of reproduction—sexual and asexual—and your child will learn both. Sexual reproduction requires two parents, while asexual reproduction does not.

Terms likely to arise during a discussion of **sexual reproduction** include:

Ovum/Egg—The female gamete, or reproductive cell.

Sperm—The male gamete, or reproductive cell.

Fertilization—The union of a sperm cell with an egg cell to form a new cell that will develop into an individual.

Zygote—A fertilized egg in its earliest stage, before it develops into an embryo.

Embryo—A developing offspring, nurtured in the womb or in an egg, before birth or hatching.

Gestation—The period of development of an offspring in its mother's womb from fertilization through birth.

Terms likely to arise during a discussion of **asexual reproduction** are as follows:

Parthenogenesis—The development of an egg into an offspring without any contribution from male sex cells. Some fish do this.

Self-fertilization—Reproduction method in which an animal possessing both male and female sex cells fertilizes itself.

Hermaphrodite—An animal (a tapeworm is one example) that has both male and female reproductive organs. Not all hermaphrodites self-fertilize, but some do.

Fragmentation—Reproduction method in which parts of an organism simply break off and become their own organism. Jellyfish can reproduce this way.

Cells and Genetics

While the Big Picture is important in life sciences and biology, your child will have to learn about cells at some point, probably later rather than sooner in his junior high career. **Cells** are the basic unit of life, the smallest part of an organism that is capable of reproducing itself. All living creatures are composed of different kinds of cells. We humans have skin cells, heart cells, blood cells, and brain cells, to name a few, while plants have root cells, leaf cells, and other cells. Here is a rundown of some of the basic organelles of both plant and animal cells:

Membrane—This is a thin layer that encloses a cell. This layer is usually **permeable**, which means that matter can pass through it. In a human cell, the membrane allows water and sugars to pass through. Plant cell walls are made out of a substance called cellulose. This differs from animal cell membranes, which are composed of fat and protein molecules.

Nucleus—Just like the atomic nucleus clubhouse, the cell nucleus—the tiny round body that controls the cell's activities—has all the neatest stuff. Most important, the nucleus contains **chromosomes,** tiny structures comprised mostly of proteins and deoxyribonucleic acid, commonly referred to as DNA. **DNA** is a large molecule that holds the genetic information of the cell, or its inheritance. The DNA in a cell determines all the features of the organism.

Cytoplasm—Cytoplasm is technically everything in a cell outside of the nucleus, but sometimes the word is used to refer to the gooey stuff that all the organelles float around in. The actual term for this jelly-like substance is **cytosol**.

Lysosome—These are tiny sacs that function as a cell's "stomach," so to speak. Lysosomes break down proteins for cellular digestion.

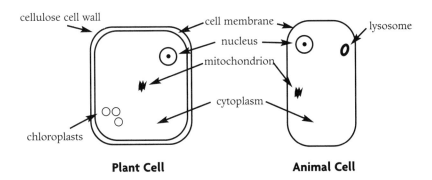

Plant Cell   **Animal Cell**

Mitochondrion—These tiny structures found in the cytoplasm function as the cell's "power station," changing food to energy.

Chloroplast—Found in plant cells, these structures contain chlorophyll. The presence of chlorophyll is necessary for photosynthesis—the conversion of sunlight into energy—to occur (see page 124).

Vacuole—These are the storage areas of a cell. Vacuoles are found in both plant and animal cells. In plant cells they are filled with cell sap. In animal cells, vacuoles store fat, among other things.

There are other cell structures, but your child is unlikely to encounter them until high school. Understanding the functions of the cell parts should be sufficient for most biology homework tasks.

Earth and Space Sciences

A more precise name for this branch of study would be "Questions About What Makes Up the Earth and How Celestial Objects—Especially the Sun, Earth, and Moon—Interact With Each Other." That would take half the class period to say, so science teachers stick with smaller titles like Geology and Astronomy, both of which fall under the banner *Earth and Space Sciences.*

Geology

Basic geology questions ask about the composition of the earth, such as, "What is the center of the earth made of?" Snack enthusiasts might answer, "A rich, creamy filling," but sadly, the correct answer is "a large ball of semi-molten metal." In this sense, you can envision the earth as a monstrous dirt-covered piece of candy, but even if you had jaws big enough to bite into it, you shouldn't, since the center contains a very nasty surprise. Here is a cross-section diagram of Earth.

Cross Section of Earth

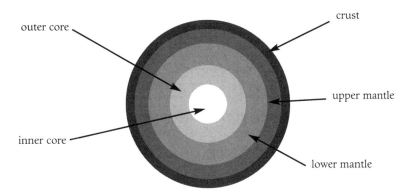

Here are the fundamental terms your child will encounter when studying geology:

Composition of the Earth

There are three layers of the earth:

Crust—The outermost solid layer of the earth. There are two types of crust, oceanic and continental. The oceanic crust resides under the ocean, and is about six miles thick. The continental crust (what we stand on) is between twenty-five and forty-five miles in width.

Mantle—The layer of rock between the crust and the core. The mantle comprises about eighty percent of the earth's volume, and is over two thousand miles thick.

Core—The central portion of the earth (below the mantle) is made up primarily of an iron-nickel alloy. The outer core is liquid, while the inner core is solid, and the temperature of the core is estimated at over 7,000 degrees Fahrenheit. (However, no one has ever gone down to the core and actually proved that there's no rich creamy filling, so snack lovers still have reason to hope.)

Tectonic Plates and the Things They Do

While your child is probably familiar with the idea of continents, a key distinction in geology is to think about tectonic plates. **Tectonic plates** are large portions of rigid rock just below the earth's surface. The continents and some of the ocean's floor rest on tectonic plates. Here's the kicker: These plates are moving! Not very fast, mind you: you won't have a tectonic plate sneak up on you while you are taking a nap in the park. However, tectonic plates are all in motion, and since the outermost level of the earth (that's the part we live on, eh?) is composed entirely of tectonic plates, this movement causes:

Mountains—A raised portion of the earth's surface that's formed when two tectonic plates collide below the surface and one pushes the other one up.

Volcanoes—An opening in the surface of the earth from which melted rock and gases flow; the material that flows out often builds up around the hole to form a mountain.

Valleys—When two tectonic plates are moving apart, they cause depressions in the earth's surface, and valleys like the Great Rift Valley are created.

Earthquakes—A shaking or movement of the earth's surface, caused by the sudden shifting or rubbing together of tectonic plates. The place where the plates are rubbing is known as a **fault line.** The fault line in Southern California is one example.

Rock Types

When you think about geology, you have to think about rocks. There are three main types:

Sedimentary—Rocks formed by the compression of particles that have settled at the bottom of rivers, lakes, and oceans. Limestone is a good example: it's formed from the compression of the remains of sea creatures.

Igneous—Rocks formed from very hot liquid matter, such as magma, that has cooled and solidified. Granite is one example.

Metamorphic—Formed when high pressure and heat meet with a sedimentary or igneous rock, resulting in a change in composition. Marble is formed by the metamorphic effects of heat and pressure on limestone.

The Atmosphere and Our Weather

Moving out from the interior of the earth, you have the air that encloses this planet, a nice little blanket known as the atmosphere. Most of the atmosphere is composed of nitrogen (seventy-eight percent) and oxygen (twenty-one percent). Important concepts about the atmosphere that might be covered in your child's homework include:

Atmospheric Pressure—This is the weight of the air pushing down on the earth, and it's measured by a barometer.

Clouds—Clouds are masses of condensed water vapor. If they are low-lying, they are called fog or mist. Your child may be asked to learn to recognize types of clouds (such as cirrus, cumulus, stratus, and thunderheads) by their shapes, their height from the ground, and the kind of precipitation they contain.

Greenhouse Effect—The greenhouse effect occurs when the sun's heat hits the earth's surface and is subsequently released, but can't escape the atmosphere because it is trapped by gasses like carbon dioxide and methane. Fossil-fuel consumption increased the level of these "greenhouse gases" in our atmosphere. It is theorized that the greenhouse effect is causing the earth to become gradually warmer, a process called **global warming.**

Ozone layer—Ozone is an oxygen-based substance that occurs in the upper atmosphere, the top layers. Ozone acts as a screen to prevent excessive amounts of ultraviolet rays from reaching Earth, which is good for humans since these rays cause skin cancer. The ozone layer is a region of high ozone concentration that exists above the earth at altitudes between ten and fifteen miles.

Precipitation—Water that falls from the air as rain, sleet, snow, and hail.

Temperature—When talking about weather, temperature refers to the degree of hotness or coldness of the air. Air temperature has a big impact on the movement of **air masses,** which are large bodies of air with only small variations in temperatures and levels of humidity, or moisture. The meeting of air masses of different characteristics causes much of our weather.

Wind patterns—To understand wind, think back to the definition of a gas. The atmosphere is composed of particles, and if you have more particles in one area than another, you have a high-pressure area (the greater number of molecules creates pressure). Like people moving from a crowded apartment to an empty house, particles like to go where they have some elbow-room. When air particles travel from a high-pressure area to a low-pressure area, you get wind.

Wind plays a large part in the earth's climates. For instance, look at a globe and you will see that most of the world's deserts occur around either thirty degrees north or thirty degrees south latitude. Winds push clouds, and if the clouds don't have rain, you get desert.

When studying geology, atmosphere, and the weather, your child is likely to encounter "what if" questions that require her to show that she understands the relationships between the forces and cycles of the earth. For example:

EXAMPLE:
Give one example each of how human activities change Earth's land, oceans, and atmosphere.

If your child presents you with a question like this, your first step should be to figure out the type of answer the teacher wants, and you can do this by looking through your child's notebook or textbook. For example, your child's teacher may have been talking about the environmental impact of things like deforestation (the cutting down of large numbers of trees), farming, irrigation, sewage, and carbon monoxide emission from cars. Once you see the kinds of terms she has been working with, help your child think of examples. Ask her questions like:

- What are some of the things humans do to the land?

- Can the resources humans use to make these products be replaced?

- What products do humans make that go into the atmosphere?

- What human products go into the ocean?

Once she answers these questions, help her think of some of the ways these actions and products affect the environment. For instance, she may decide to talk about how cutting down the Amazon Rainforest might reduce the amount of oxygen in our atmosphere.

Astronomy

As stated earlier, the bulk of junior high astronomy will focus on how the earth, sun, and moon interact with each other. Tell your child it's like an episode of MTV's *The Real World,* only it's on a galactic scale and the sun never breaks down crying because the moon is being unfriendly.

If you look back to the discussion of gravity on pages 121-122, you will remember that bodies with mass create gravitational forces. Well, the sun's the biggest thing in this solar system, and Earth and all the other planets are caught in its gravitational pull. This causes our planet to rotate around the sun.

If the sun's size is making you feel insecure, or you're angry that the earth is trapped in its orbit when the sun didn't even ask permission, just keep in mind that the earth is much larger than the moon. The earth's gravitational force is what keeps the moon in orbit around us. The moon's gravitational force affects us in the form of tides.

Before discussing eclipses and seasons, you should gather together a table lamp, an orange, and a golf ball, or objects that are similar to these. A problem your child, and many people, may have with astronomy is that the topics being explained are just so large. Envisioning the earth, sun, moon, and all the other planets spinning around in huge cosmic orbits can cause a headache. This brings about a famous bit of advice:

When discussing astronomy, always keep a good supply of spherically shaped fruit around. When the homework is over, eat the planets.

Explaining the Solar System

The Earth (orange) travels around the Sun (lamp) in an ellipse, which is like a flattened circle. The Earth is tilted, so draw a horizontal line around the middle of the orange to represent the equator and then shift it at a slight angle.

Earth Orbiting the Sun

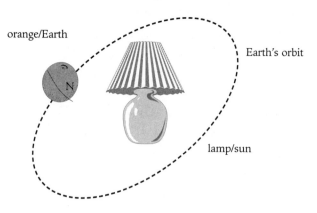

orange/Earth

Earth's orbit

lamp/sun

Once you do this, you see that more sunlight is falling on the northern half of the orange than the southern half. This causes summer in the northern part of the earth and winter in the southern part. If you move the orange around 180 degrees, you get the opposite situation. This leads to summer in the southern part of the world and winter in the northern part.

At the equator, it's pretty much hot all the time.

Now, bring that golf ball of a moon into play. With the moon spinning around the earth, you can place the moon between the earth and the sun. Ta da! You have created a solar **eclipse**, the partial or total darkening of one celestial body by its passage through the shadow of another. The moon doesn't stay in the path of the sun for long, though, as it travels about 2,000 miles per hour.

Long-Term Science Projects and the Scientific Method

Many long-term science projects involve setting up an experiment and drawing conclusions from the results.

Suppose your child came up to you after dinner and proclaimed, "I want to be the greatest mad scientist the world has ever known." Rather than reminding him that mad scientists only exist in old black-and-white movies, you should praise him for his lofty goals and then send him off to study the Scientific Method (also known as scientific inquiry).

The Scientific Method

1. Pose a question.

This is similar to coming up with a good main idea for an English essay. Consider a life sciences experiment in which your child will test various fertilizers to see which one works best with bean plants. The question in this scientific experiment would be, "Which of these three fertilizers—eggshells, cough medicine, or plastic action figurines—

works best to help bean plants grow?" Your child would then set up a scientific experiment to try and answer this question.

2. Suggest a plausible answer/Develop a hypothesis.

A **hypothesis** is an educated guess that can be tested. So to develop a hypothesis for the fertilizer experiment, you could say, "The cough medicine will help the plants the most; since it makes people feel better, it should make bean plants feel better." This might not be the best guess, but it isn't crucial to have the correct hypothesis every time. The results of your experiment will either confirm or deny your hypothesis, so you can always revise your hypothesis in light of any new evidence uncovered.

3. Test the idea by conducting an experiment.

This is the key aspect of the scientific method. Your child must set up his experiment so that only the main question is being tested.

To do this in the bean plant fertilizer experiment, brainstorm with your child about all the different variables that could affect plant growth. You might come up with a list that contains many of these variables:

1) Amount of sunlight received

2) Amount of water received

3) Type of soil

4) Amount of soil in pot

5) Amount of exposure plant has to Tibbles, the plant-eating cat

6) Type of fertilizer used

These six variables all affect bean plant growth, but your child's experiment is interested only in number 6, the type of fertilizer. Therefore, to make this a proper scientific experiment, you must ensure that the other five factors are equal among the test plants in order for the results to have any meaning.

This means each test plant receives the exact same amount of sunlight and water, is planted in the same type of soil, has the same amount of soil, and is protected from Tibbles equally. With these five factors all equal, the remaining factor is "type of fertilizer." Therefore, any difference in plant growth between the test plants can be attributed to the different fertilizers used.

The correct set-up for this experiment would consist of four plants in identical pots, with identical soil, given similar amounts of sunlight and water. Plant 1 would receive four grams of eggshells each day (placed in the soil), Plant 2 would get four grams of cough medicine, while Plant 3 would receive four grams of plastic action figure placed in its soil. The results of each plant's growth would be measured each day—at the same time every day—for a period of two weeks.

You may have noticed that there are four plants total, but only Plants 1-3 receive fertilizer. Plant 4 illustrates the idea of a control group. A **control group** is a group in an experiment that is not manipulated. In this experiment, no fertilizer is given to the control group plant so that your child can discover how a plant would grow without the effect of any fertilizer. In this experiment, a control group is important because it helps your child determine whether any of the fertilizers actually aid growth.

4. Record results and determine whether hypothesis is correct.

After two weeks, your child will have collected data on the growth of four bean plants. Let's suppose his final results were the following:

Plant 1 (eggshells)	10 inches
Plant 2 (cough medicine)	2 inches
Plant 3 (plastic)	7 inches
Plant 4 (control)	7 inches

With these results, you can see that the original hypothesis was not correct: cough medicine was not the best fertilizer. However, if riginally, Socrates divided this step into two steps: (1) Accept the hypothesis as provisionally true, and then (2) Act accordingly. Our method is modified towards a scientific experiment as homework assignment, but in essence both methods are similar.

your child modified his hypothesis to state, "Egg shells help fertilize bean plants better than cough medicine or plastic," and then ran the experiment again, he would find his hypothesis to be provisionally true. (The word provisionally is used because this is the result of only one experiment, so we haven't proved that it is true all the time, every time.)

Having a control group plant lets your child make further statements. Since the plastic-fed plant grew at the same rate as the control group plant, you could conclude that plastic had no effect on bean plant growth rate. If you did not have a control group, there would be no way to make this statement. Furthermore, since you know that a bean plant with no fertilizer would have grown seven inches, and the cough medicine plant only grew two inches, you can state that "Our experiment showed that cough medicine was harmful to bean plant growth." You have the data from the experiment to back this statement up provisionally (it could be that only the amount of cough medicine caused harmful effects, and that smaller doses could still be beneficial).

Reporting the Results of an Experiment

At this point, your child will have completed a successful experiment using the scientific method. This might be sufficient in itself, but in the later grades she will probably be asked to write up the results of her experiment. This would include a brief report about the structure of the experiment and the results, as well as a chart or graph representing the results.

Writing the Report

Your child's report can be brief and can follow the structure of the scientific method itself. The first paragraph would describe the question being addressed; the second paragraph would describe the hypothesis; the third paragraph would describe the experimental design; and the fourth paragraph would describe the results of the experiment. If the results were inconclusive, your child might use a fifth paragraph to describe possible new approaches to answering the original question.

Representing Data

A simple chart or graph is usually all that is needed to represent the results of an experiment. For example, we might represent the results of our plant experiment using a line graph showing the growth rate of our plants over two weeks.

CHAPTER 5

A Review of Key Junior High Social Studies Concepts

 **JUNIOR HIGH SOCIAL STUDIES COVERS** civics, economics, geography, and history. These are all large topics, and we can't summarize them completely in this chapter. Instead, we will give you a quick refresher and a framework for approaching these topics, examples of the kinds of homework questions your child might encounter, and tips for addressing those questions.

Civics

*I*n this section, we will discuss the ideal model for how the American government is supposed to work, although sometimes your child's classroom discussions revolve around whether the government *actually* works that way. In America, we consider the ideal model of government to be a **democracy**, a system of government in which the people hold ultimate power and select their government representatives (the people who run the government) in free elections.

Three pieces of parchment have had a great impact on our democracy: the Declaration of Independence, the Constitution, and the Bill of Rights.

The Declaration of Independence

This document is important because it announced the creation of a separate, new nation known as the United States. It was written chiefly by Thomas Jefferson in 1776, which was at the beginning of the American Revolution against England.

The Declaration states that all men are created equal, and that everyone has the right to life, liberty, and the pursuit of happiness.

The United States Constitution

This document was created and ratified after the U.S. had won its independence from England. All thirteen states had ratified it by 1789. The Articles of the Constitution established the United States government and its system of laws, and it is the system of government that we still use today. The Constitution defines the rights to which all Americans are entitled, and describes the three main branches of government:

Executive Branch—This branch includes the President and Vice President of the U.S., but it also includes all Cabinet members and agencies, which are appointed by the President. The function of the executive branch is to carry out laws passed by the legislative branch.

Watching the news, or reading the news daily (either on the Internet or in a newspaper), will help your child with his social studies work. Many current events are covered in history classes, since a current political situation can often be explained in light of past events. You can encourage your child to watch the news by explaining to him that people who are completely uninformed about the world around them often do not get the job/scholarship/date with significant other/new car that they want.

Legislative Branch—This is the U.S. Congress, which is a **bicameral** body since it is composed of two separate houses, the Senate and the House of Representatives. The function of Congress is to make laws.

Judicial Branch—This includes the Supreme Court, the highest court in the country, as well as the other courts throughout the country. The function of the judicial branch is to explain and apply the laws passed by the legislative branch.

Division of Power

The Constitution also describes how the three branches of government must work together. This is called the **system of checks and balances**, a division of the powers of the different branches of our government that is designed to insure that no one branch of the government can become too strong and overpower the others. A good analogy to this is the rock/scissors/paper game you play with your hand if you need to decide who has to get up and bring in more snacks when your family is watching a movie. In the game, rock beats scissors, but loses to paper. Each item is strong in some way, but can be defeated by another item.

This is our government in a nutshell. Each branch of government has its powers, but these powers can be checked by the other branches in specific ways. The President, for example, can sign a treaty with a foreign country, but the Senate can refuse to sign the treaty. Similarly, Congress can pass a law, but the President can **veto**, or reject, it. However, if Congress can pass the law with a two-thirds majority in both houses, it becomes a law anyway . . . unless the Supreme Court decides that the law is **unconstitutional**—not in keeping with the principles laid out in the Constitution—in which case it gets tossed into the dumpster.

*Could your child learn all this information merely by watching **The West Wing**? Sadly, no, but it is still a good show.*

In fact, there is a system of checks and balances within Congress itself. There are 100 members of the Senate, two for each state, and they serve for six years. There are 435 members of the House of Representatives, and they serve for two years. The number of representatives from each state is determined by each state's population, so California has many more representatives than Alaska. You would think that this would allow them to pass California-friendly, Alaska-harmful bills whenever they want. This would work in the House, but when it reached the Senate, the two Senators from Alaska would evenly match the two Senators from California, giving them an opportunity to prevent the bill from passing.

As you look at the big picture, you can see that this system is designed so that laws can only be passed if all three branches of government are willing to work together.

Division of Power, Part II: Federal and State Powers

Our government is founded on a belief in **federalism**, which is a system of government wherein power is shared between national and state governments. Both the national and state governments have exclusive powers (meaning that the other one doesn't have that power), such as the power of the federal government to regulate interstate trade and declare war, or the power of the state governments to issue licenses and regulate intrastate trade. Our national and state governments also share powers, such as the power to collect taxes, build roads, and enforce laws. So while our government today places most of its power in the hands of Congress, the President, and the Supreme Court, their powers can be checked by those of the states, and vice-versa.

While the Articles of the Constitution describe how government should be structured, the Constitution also contains . . .

The Bill of Rights

This is the third of the Big Three Government Pieces of Paper, and it contains the first ten amendments to the Constitution. The Bill of Rights defines the rights and freedoms of American citizens in relation to their government. These include all your favorite Amendments, such as the right to free speech, the right to choose your own religion, and the right not to incriminate yourself. In subsequent years, seventeen new amendments have been added.

Political Parties

Any government in which two or more political parties compete for power is considered a **multi-party system** of government. Our country has two main political parties—the Democrats and the Republicans—but there are other smaller parties, such as the Green Party. We in America consider multi-party systems a good thing because, like our system of checks and balances, multiple parties provide added insurance that no one person or group will become too powerful. If a representative of one party does something Americans don't like, they can simply vote for a person from another party at the next election.

The Media

Traditionally, the governmental role of the media—the media includes all information vehicles, including newspapers, magazines, pamphlets, movies, radio, television, and, yes, even textbooks—has been to let the public know about the current political arguments and events, good and bad, in government. Also, since most people will never meet the President, the media helps keep the general public aware of what he is saying and doing in Washington, D.C. However, some people consider the media to be the "fourth branch" of government, because it has the ability to exert such an influence on American opinions (particularly since television became widespread). When studying the Vietnam War, for example, your child will probably learn how nightly televised reports and pictures of the conflict overseas led many Americans to join the anti-war movement.

Learning about civics requires good, old-fashioned memorization along with the ability to draw some conclusions about the way our government works. Here are some examples of the types of homework questions your child might see:

EXAMPLE:

Who were the main framers of the Constitution and what roles did they play in drafting and ratifying the document?

This is a straight historical question that requires little independent thought. The goal is to get your child to memorize the names and actions of our founding fathers. The information your child needs to answer this question will probably be in her notes or textbook. If not, a quick search in the encyclopedia will reveal the answer.

EXAMPLE:

Compare the government of the Roman Empire with the American government of today.

This type of question requires more careful consideration, as it is asking your child to either draw on a previously learned body of knowledge or do some research. The first step in tackling a compare/contrast social studies question is for your child to get all the facts in front of her. In this case, your child might need to use an outside source, such as an encyclopedia or educational CD-ROM, to learn a little about Roman government.

The second step of the question is to align key similarities and differences. For example, citizens of the Roman Empire voted, as do citizens of the U.S.; however, your child will learn that the definition of "citizen" in the Roman Empire is not the same as it is in contemporary America. Only a privileged class of men were allowed to vote in ancient Rome.

The third step of the question is to organize a response. For example, your child might choose to examine differences first, then discuss similarities. Or vice versa. As long as there is a clear structure, it doesn't matter what order the comparison follows.

Economics

Your child will probably not have a homework assignment focused entirely on economics, but a great deal of history contains economic components, so it is important to know and understand the basic terms. Let us begin by first talking about economics on a small scale, and then move up to the economics of countries.

Microeconomics

The centerpiece of microeconomics is the **law of supply and demand**, which determines the price of an object. **Supply** means how many of a particular good or service are available for purchase. **Demand** refers to how many people wish to purchase a particular good or service. Let us use silkworms and roaches as an example. Suppose your child wanted to go into business selling these two insects as pets. He discovers that many people like the idea of making their own silk (although technically the worm's going to do all the work), so the demand for silkworms is high. In fact, the demand is much greater than the supply of silkworms, and your child realizes that he can charge twice as much for each silkworm and still find takers.

Therefore, since demand exceeds supply, the price of an item increases. On the other side, no one is interested in buying cockroaches. And unfortunately, there are a lot of cockroaches. Since the supply of cockroaches exceeds demand, the price of cockroaches will fall, probably all the way down to 100 cockroaches for $0.01.

The United States—and most of the world, for that matter—now use money as a means of currency, so prices will refer to dollars and cents. However, it was not always this way. Early human civilizations used **barter**, the exchange of one item for another, instead of money, so one pig might be worth five jars of olive oil. Even so, the law of supply and demand still operated, since an increase in demand for pigs would lead to a change in the exchange rate: say, one pig might now get you eight jars of olive oil.

So if your child is reading an article about a postwar country, and he learns that people will wait in line for three hours to buy bread at high prices, what does he know about bread in the postwar economy? He should realize that demand greatly exceeds supply, and that the country's economy is probably very weak, since it is having trouble supplying basic foodstuffs.

If your child is ever given an assignment that deals with some conflict in history, there is usually an economic element to it. Societies don't go to war for kicks: typically some resource or commodity is at stake, and one group wants to control the supply and not let the other side have it. This sort of struggle is called **competition** when it is between two rival hot dogs stands fighting for the same customers, but once the hot dog stand owners raise armies, the competition becomes war.

EXAMPLE:

Maya Root Coffeehouse has been in business in Centerville for 20 years serving a small selection of imported coffee drinks for $3 a cup. It has enjoyed a limited, but devoted, clientele. Last month, a new Ishmael Coffee Stand shop—one of a national chain of over 500 Ishmael Coffee Stands—opened down the block offering a wide variety of imported coffee drinks for $2 a cup. What economic impact might this have on Maya Root?

This is the kind of question your child's teacher might give him to test whether he understands supply and demand. While no one can completely predict public behavior, certain assumptions can be made about the situation described above. There is no perfectly right answer to this question, but as long as your child can use microeconomic principles to support himself, he should be fine.

When your child is having trouble answering a question like this, you can help him by asking leading questions. Using the example above, some appropriate leading questions might be:

- Why do you think Maya Root's clientele was so small to begin with?

- If Maya Root's clientele was so small, why do you think it stayed in business?

- Do you think the prices offered by Ishmael's will make a difference in the number of customers it attracts?

- What kinds of things can Maya Root do to become competitive?

These types of questions will help your child pick out the important elements provided in the question, and then expand upon them to develop a response.

Macroeconomics

In microeconomics, when one company makes eight million dollars in one year selling wicker chairs, that is its **annual revenue**. When you add up the monetary value of all the goods and services created in one country during a specified period of time, you have that country's **gross national product**, or **GNP**. The difference is primarily one of scale. The GNP is a good indicator of the economic health of a country. If everyone in the country keeps doing better on average, the GNP will increase. During a time like the Great Depression, the GNP fell, indicating that America's economy was suffering.

Besides GNP, two other important items that governments watch are inflation and unemployment. If the average price of all goods and services produced in a country increases from one year to the next, or if the purchasing power of money decreases, you have **inflation**. Inflation becomes a national problem if prices go up but everyone's earnings stay the same, because they will be unable to buy as much with the same amount of money as they used to.

Therefore, tell your child to think of inflation as similar to eating cheescake. A little bit of cheesecake every year won't kill you, but if

The stock market is another indicator of the economic health of a country. Once again, the law of supply and demand comes into play. People buy stock—which gives them a percentage of ownership in a corporation—based on its current price. They buy the stock because they believe the company will continue to make money into the future; by owning a part of the company, they will be able to share in the profits. Demand for stock in a company will lead to an increase in that company's stock prices, so if the stock market is going up, this means people have confidence that there is money and profit to be made in the future. On the other hand, if people think that they own stock in a company that is going downhill (think of a typewriter company right after the personal computer became popular), they will try to sell off their stock. Overall, the stock market indexes will show this sell-off with a drop in value.

cheesecake eating increases greatly, your economy (your pants size) is going to feel the strain.

Inflation and other financial woes often lead to high **unemployment**, which as you might think, means "not working a job, although capable of working one." That second part is there because two-year-olds are not unemployed, they are just toddlers in diapers. Governments tend to be concerned with unemployment for two reasons:

1) Often, the government has to provide for the unemployed, which means raising money, usually in the form of taxes.

2) Governments who do not or cannot provide for their unemployed citizens are left with a large number of hungry people with a lot of free time on their hands; historically, this has led to things like revolutions.

These basic economic principles will give your child the foundation he needs to understand many historical events.

Common Economic Terms

In addition to the ideas already discussed, the following economic terms may also prove helpful:

Production and Consumption—Something that is made is **produced**, while something used or ingested is **consumed**. Production is often used on a large scale, to say something like, "Production of tiny cars has vastly exceeded consumers' current needs." This is just another way of saying that tiny car makers made a lot of tiny cars that no one wanted to buy.

Goods and Services—In general, all jobs can be placed into one of these categories. **Goods** are anything that's created that someone wants or needs; doughnuts, tires, squeaky shoes, and paintings of dogs playing poker are all examples of goods produced. A **service** is the performance of work for someone else. For example, providing financial advice, medical care, and tutoring sessions are all services.

Entrepreneurs—These are people who strike out on their own to create, organize, manage—and assume the risk for—their own company. Entrepreneurs are often people who create businesses that are different from existing ones. The first automobile maker was an entrepreneur who decided to create a new product that people would use for transportation instead of their horse.

Tariffs—Duties (taxes) imposed by a government on imports or exports. When Government A wants to protect an industry in its own country, let's say steel, it places a tariff on all steel imported into Country A.

Geography

Geography is not just about memorizing state capitals and looking at maps. The people and things on the maps also fall under the heading of geography to some degree, as we will discuss.

Maps and General Map Skills

Maps provide a much-needed visual component to historical events, which is why geography is so important in grades six through eight. While a globe will show the actual distance Columbus traveled, other maps can provide students with a wealth of information. To help your child with his social studies, then, there are two main duties you should try to fulfill.

1. Provide him with access to maps.

If your child has a computer in his study area, then a map CD-ROM is an excellent purchase. Whatever area of the world your child is studying, he can punch it up on the computer screen to view it. This will help him understand the events, as it is much easier to visualize "the armies moved from France to Belgium" if he has a map of Europe in front of him.

*I**f you get a CD-ROM map, it is a good idea to get a CD-ROM that provides a variety of information besides just political boundaries. Some CD-ROMs will have maps showing population densities, educational levels, birth rates, and other data. This will help your child learn more about a country.*

If your child doesn't have access to a computer, that is not a problem. However, your child should have a good atlas or some form of fold-out world map or globe that he can refer to if necessary. Some maps are quite nice, and make great posters for a study area. Even if your child starts avoiding homework by staring at the map, at least he will be learning geography at some level.

2. Help your child analyze the information on a map.

Many maps come chock full of information: political boundaries, rivers, mountain ranges, major roads, deserts, swamps, airports, electrical substations, national parks, intermittent salt lakes, and capitals are all marked in an area the size of your hand. If your child's homework requires him to interpret this information and he's having difficulty, then the first place to look is the key. Every map and globe has a **key** that explains how everything is ordered.

The key often contains symbols, and these symbols vary from map to map.

But if you and your child take it one question at a time, map questions should not be overwhelming. If the question talks about how many miles it is from Point Q to City R, you will need to use the **map scale**, which shows how many miles equals one inch on the map. Then it is just a matter of getting your child to use the ruler he keeps in his homework area to measure the distance in inches and then convert it to miles.

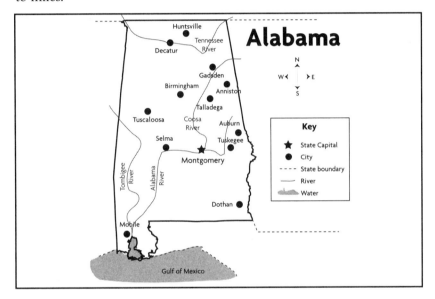

EXAMPLE:

On the map provided, draw a circle around the capital of Alabama, and make a list of all rivers shown.

This is a question about map reading. As mentioned before, the first step is to check the key, which reveals that state capitals are marked with a star. Your child just needs to search for and circle the star to answer this part of the question correctly. The key also reveals that rivers are marked by dotted lines. Your child now needs to look for the dotted lines and the names written over them and make a list of all the names he sees.

EXAMPLE:

Create a map of your neighborhood. Your map must include a scale and a key.

This type of geography problem is a little more difficult and is unlikely to appear before the eighth grade. To help your child become an expert cartographer, use the same approach as you would for a long-term project: get him to decide on many of the factors before starting, so that he will have a clear idea of what his map should look like. What features should he include? How should he indicate roads, highways, and bodies of water? Examples of how to do all of these things can be found on other maps, so he does not have to invent a brand-new system on his own. Your child just needs to decide how his map will look—in effect, he is creating his own key at this stage—and then place it down on paper.

The People and Places on Maps

Geography overlaps with other branches of social science when it comes to understanding how the landscape affects things like immigration and boundary squabbles. The main principle to keep in mind here is the one that real estate agents still swear by: Location, Location, Location! Folks want the best goodies for themselves and their pals, so they usually try to set up cities and countries in the best possible location. A "good" location usually means: plenty of space for farming on fertile soil; access to water for drinking and irrigation; access to the sea so trade with other countries is easier; protection afforded by natural boundaries like mountains and oceans; valuable natural resources like lumber, gold, petroleum, and spices. Most early wars were fought over access to natural resources. Even today, countries are sometimes motivated to use force to protect their access to things like oil.

History

History homework, like most homework, comes in two general types: fact-based questions and complicated essay questions that require the formation of theories and the drawing of conclusions.

Fact-Based Questions

If your child comes to you with a very specific historical question, like "When was the Treaty of Ghent signed?" there's no use trying to bluff that you know the answer. Your child has used all the cool new excuses—and your old ones will not fool him.

Your duty is to help your child find the exact answer, and this means looking in the following places, in this order:

1. The textbook

Of course, your child will have already checked here first. Your child should be aware of whether or not his teacher assigned questions that could be found in the reading or would require research. If your child did look but just did not locate it, that's okay; if it becomes a regular occurrence this indicates that your child is not absorbing much of what he is reading. Sometimes your child forgets his textbook, so it's on to . . .

2. A general reference book or encyclopedia CD-ROM

Having a general history book with a good index can come in handy at this moment. Go to the index, look up the Treaty of Ghent, and see if you can find the answer there. A CD-ROM word search should get you the answer as well.

3. The Internet

If you have a computer, go to a search engine, type in Treaty of Ghent, and see what links pop up. It is a good idea to stick to sites that end in .edu, since these are educational sites such as colleges.

4. The library

If your child has a lot of unanswered historical questions, a trip to the library might be warranted. However, don't spend a huge chunk of time tracking down a single fact unless your child has developed a quest-like fervor for the answer. Spending an entire evening searching for one answer is not an efficient use of time, especially if it breeds rancor in your child and exhaustion in you.

Essay Questions

Complicated history questions are much like complicated English questions. They ask your child to approach an historical topic from a certain point of view or to compare certain historical events. The same principles for addressing literary analysis questions apply here (see pages 93-100).

Long-Term Social Studies Projects

Long-term social studies projects are usually long papers focused on history. They require research, writing, and grammar skills, so the approach discussed on pages 104-111 will work well here.

Your child may also be asked to draw on different types of research materials to complete a project. These materials are usually broken down into two categories:

Primary Sources—Primary sources are things like historical documents, interviews, letters, and diaries. These are actual historical artifacts that have not been interpreted or explained by a critic or scholar.

Secondary Sources—These are things like scholarly books and articles. Secondary sources offer explanations and interpretations of events and materials and usually rely on primary sources for back-up. Authors of secondary source material may also rely on other secondary sources.

Using secondary source material is a skill your child has been learning for some time. Every time she looks up something in the encyclopedia, she is using a secondary source. Using primary sources is trickier and more advanced because it will require your child to make her own judgments about the meaning and importance of a particular document or historical event. Instead of relying solely on scholarly articles about Martin Luther King Jr.'s political beliefs to write a school paper, for example, she may be asked to use his letters and transcripts of his speeches to form her own opinion. She should follow the same guidelines offered for interpreting literary works on pages 93-100.

CHAPTER 6

Fencing Lessons
and A Final Word

MANY STUDENTS WILL NEED HELP on topics that fall outside of the major areas covered in this book. If your child is taking fencing lessons, for example, we really have not given you any pointers to pass on to him. Okay, here's one—keep your elbow extended when lunging—but that's it. Our fencing days are over.

If your child's homework assignment consists of learning to play the scales on his French horn, don't worry that you have never picked up the instrument in your life. In this case, and in others, you won't be able to impart the correct knowledge to him at a moment's notice. But regardless of the subject matter, when your child asks you for help on his homework you can always be supportive, caring, and kind when answering. If you don't know the answer, and the two of you search and can't find the answer, don't get frustrated and upset. Keep in mind there's a larger issue at stake, which is the relationship between you and your child.

Mutual caring and respect between the two of you will always be more important than any one fact, so if you find yourself losing your composure because you and your child cannot find out what year the Treaty of Ghent was signed, don't get upset. Reassure your child that homework doesn't have to be perfect every time, and you can always learn from your mistakes. This positive, caring attitude—more than any one fact—is what will make you a homework hero in the eyes of your child.

By the way, the Treaty of Ghent was signed in 1814.

Homework on the World Wide Web

If you have a computer with an Internet connection, you might like to take a peek at these homework-related sites:

Bigchalk.com
http://www.bigchalk.com

B.J. Pinchbeck's Homework Helper
http://school.discovery.com/homeworkhelp/bjpinchbeck/index.html

Dictionary.com
http://www.dictionary.com

DiscoverySchool.com
http://school.discovery.com/students/

Fact Monster.com
http://www.factmonster.com/homework/

Homeworkspot.com
http://www.homeworkspot.com/

Thesaurus.com
http://www.thesaurus.com/

Yahooligans! School Bell: Homework Help
http://www.yahooligans.com/school_bell/homework_help/

Information for parents of children with learning differences
http://www.SchwabLearning.com

Other Books by Priscilla L. Vail, M.A.T.

A Language Yardstick: Understanding and Assessment
About Dyslexia: Unraveling the Myth
Clear and Lively Writing: Language Games and Activities for Everyone
Common Ground: Phonics and Whole Language Working Together
Emotion: The On/Off Switch for Learning
Gifted, Precocious, or Just Plain Smart
Learning Styles: Food for Thought and 130 Practical Tips
Reading Comprehension: Students' Needs and Teachers' Tools
Smart Kids with School Problems: Things to Know and Ways to Help
Third and Fourth Grade Language Assessment
Words Fail Me!: How Language Works and What Happens When It Doesn't
The World of the Gifted Child

Acknowledgements

Drew and Cynthia Johnson would like to thank their friends—Frank, Jeff, Renee, John, Sam, and Kelly—at Magnolia Café South and Vulcan Video South for keeping them well-fed and visually entertained during the course of writing this book.